The New York Concert Saloon
The Devil's Own Nights

In this book Brooks McNamara explores the world of the concert saloon in New York from the Civil War to the early years of the twentieth century. A concert saloon is defined as an establishment offering various kinds of entertainment, including alcohol, with some also providing gambling and prostitution. All of these saloons employed "waiter girls" to sell drinks and sit with male customers, and all had bad reputations. Focusing on the theatrical aspects of the concert saloon, McNamara examines the sources of saloon shows, the changes in direction during the century, and the performing spaces and equipment, as well as the employees and patrons. He paints a picture of a lively and theatrically fascinating environment, and his work sheds new light on our understanding of American popular theatre. The book contains informative illustrations and will be of interest to historians of theatre, popular culture, and American social history.

BROOKS MCNAMARA is Professor of Performance Studies, Emeritus, in the Tisch School of the Arts at New York University; and Director, Emeritus of the Shubert Archive. He is a specialist in the history of popular entertainment and has written and published widely in the area, including *The American Playhouse in the Eighteenth Century* and *American Popular Entertainments*.

T0381911

The American theatre and its literature are attracting, after long neglect, the crucial attention of historians, theoreticians and critics of the arts. Long a field for isolated research yet too frequently marginalized in the academy, the American theatre has always been a sensitive gauge of social pressures and public issues. Investigations into its myriad of shapes and manifestations are relevant to students of drama, theatre, literature, cultural experience and political development.

The primary intent of this series is to set up a forum of important and original scholarship in and criticism of American theatre and drama in a cultural and social context. Inclusive by design, the series accommodates leading work in areas ranging from the study of drama as literature to theatre histories, theoretical explorations, production histories and readings of more popular or para-theatrical forms. While maintaining a specific emphasis on theatre in the United States, the series welcomes work grounded broadly in cultural studies and narratives with interdisciplinary reach. Cambridge Studies in American Theatre and Drama thus provides a crossroads where historical, theoretical, literary and biographical approaches meet and combine, promoting imaginative research in theatre and drama from a variety of new perspectives.

BOOKS IN THE SERIES

1. Samuel Hay, *African American Theatre*
2. Marc Robinson, *The Other American Drama*
3. Amy Green, *The Revisionist Stage: American Directors Re-Invent the Classics*
4. Jared Brown, *The Theatre in America during the Revolution*
5. Susan Harris Smith, *American Drama: The Bastard Art*
6. Mark Fearnow, *The American Stage and the Great Depression*
7. Rosemarie K. Bank, *Theatre Culture in America, 1825–1860*
8. Dale Cockrell, *Demons of Disorder: Early Blackface Minstrels and Their World*
9. Stephen J. Bottoms, *The Theatre of Sam Shepard*
10. Michael A. Morrison, *John Barrymore, Shakespearean Actor*
11. Brenda Murphy, *Congressional Theatre: Dramatizing McCarthyism on Stage, Film, and Television*
12. Jorge Huerta, *Chicano Drama: Performance, Society and Myth*
13. Roger A. Hall, *Performing the American Frontier, 1870–1906*
14. Brooks McNamara, *The New York Concert Saloon: The Devil's Own Nights*

The New York Concert Saloon
The Devil's Own Nights

BROOKS McNAMARA

New York University

CAMBRIDGE
UNIVERSITY PRESS

CAMBRIDGE UNIVERSITY PRESS
Cambridge, New York, Melbourne, Madrid, Cape Town, Singapore, São Paulo

Cambridge University Press
The Edinburgh Building, Cambridge CB2 8RU, UK

Published in the United States of America by Cambridge University Press, New York

www.cambridge.org
Information on this title: www.cambridge.org/9780521814782

First published 2002
This digitally printed version 2007

A catalogue record for this publication is available from the British Library

Library of Congress Cataloguing in Publication data
McNamara, Brooks.
The New York concert saloon : the devil's own nights / Brooks McNamara.
p.   cm. – (Cambridge studies in American theatre and drama, ISSN ; 14)
Includes bibliographical references and index.
ISBN 0 521 81478 2
1. Music-halls (Variety-theaters, cabarets, etc.) – New York (State) – New
York – History – 19th century.   I. Title.   II. Series.
PN1968.U5 M32   2002
792.7′09747′109034 – dc21   2002017388

ISBN 978-0-521-81478-2 hardback
ISBN 978-0-521-03699-3 paperback

To the late Vera Brodsky Lawrence,
a great friend and
a great historian of the music
of early New York City

Oh! The night that I struck New York,
I went out for a quiet walk;
Folks who are 'on to' the City say,
Better by far that I took Broadway;
But I was out to enjoy the sights,
There was the Bow'ry ablaze with lights;
I had one of the devil's own nights!
I'll never go there any more.

Charles H. Hoyt and Percy Gaunt,
"The Bowery," from *A Trip To Chinatown*, 1892

Contents

List of illustrations	*page* viii
Foreword	xi
Preface	xiii
Acknowledgments	xxi
Prologue: sources of the concert saloon and its shows	1
1	Where the devil's work is done: New York City concert saloons during the Civil War era	11
2	Changes in direction: the concert saloon after the war	27
3	Concert-saloon acts	41
4	Concert saloons: spaces and equipment	61
5	Employees and patrons of the concert saloon	77
6	Related forms	96
	Epilogue	117
	Appendices	123
	Notes	132
	Bibliography	136
	Index	141

Illustrations

The illustrations are from the collection of the author, except Number 8, which is from the collection of the Museum of the City of New York, and Number 5 and 6, which are from Special Collections, Brown University.

1	Wilton's Music Hall, Wellclose Square, London, n.d.	*page* 4
2	"Saturday Night on the Bowery," woodcut, *c.* 1875.	13
3	Outside "talker" at a dime museum, Harry Muhrman, *Harper's Weekly*, February 26, 1881.	14
4	Bill from a New York variety theatre, September 16, 1873.	38
5 and 6	Lithograph sheet music covers of two sentimental songs performed in concert saloons in the 1880s and published in the 1870s: "Take This Letter to My Mother" and "I Have No Home."	44/45
7	Photograph of a New York City concert saloon or variety house, n.d.	46
8	Stock poster for a concert saloon, *c.* 1860.	71
9	"A German Beer Garden in New York City on Sunday Evening," *Harper's Weekly*, October 15, 1859.	98
10	Celebrating the Capitulation of the Sedan at the "Atlantic Garden," n.d.	100
11	Flyer for Harry Hill's, 1887.	110
12	Interior of Harry Hill's, *National Police Gazette*, November 22, 1879.	112
13	Cover page of a summons issued to Harry Hill's, 1887.	114
14	Supreme Court of New York, "Affidavit of Service," Harry Hill's, 1887.	115

15   Interior of a Cheyenne concert saloon, *Frank Leslie's*
      Illustrated Newspaper, October 13, 1877.   118
16   Flyer for the extant Bird Cage Theatre, a concert
      saloon in Tombstone, Arizona.   121

Foreword

As an institution the concert saloon has been accepted for many years as an important predecessor to many forms of American popular entertainment, in particular variety and later vaudeville and burlesque. Other early locations for staged variety entertainment included beer gardens and dime museums. Concert saloons developed in the American frontier where organized entertainment was virtually nonexistent. In these rudimentary entertainment establishments the patron was offered alcohol, gambling, women, a rough and tumble atmosphere, and, as an enticement, free entertainment. Not surprisingly, the frontier concert saloon catered almost exclusively to a male audience. Concert saloons spread to major U.S. cities, and urban versions of the concert saloon prospered. The burgeoning urban population was a natural setting for enterprising saloon owners to see the potential in such venues, attracting drinking and carousing patrons with the added appeal of entertainers.

By the late 1850s and early 1860s concert saloons were well established in New York City, located primarily in the lower Broadway area and on the Bowery; but by the early 1860s most major cities had concert saloons and by the mid-1860s they were common in many smaller towns. New York City undoubtedly had the largest number in the nineteenth century – as many as 300. After the Civil War, with public outcries against the prostitution and vice so frequently associated with the concert saloon, variety began to break away from the saloon atmosphere and move into regular theatres, thus gaining a higher degree of respectability, yet for a time still offering similar fare. Even many of the surviving concert saloons in the 1870s and 1880s attempted to minimize the loathsome connotations attached to these venues – and especially the "waiter girls" who hustled drinks, warmed up to the clients, and sometimes were little more than prostitutes – by altering the identification of their facilities with such nomenclatures as music halls, concert gardens, or concert rooms, and, as Brooks McNamara illustrates, adopting impressive names for their establishments.

Yet despite the enormous significance of concert saloons in the history of entertainment in the United States, precious little has been written about them, especially in terms of what actually went on within their confines, the nature of the performances and the performers, the theatrical configurations of the spaces – some quite elaborate, most simple and basic in their accoutrements – and the structure of the establishments, the nature of their management, the profile of the patrons, and their distinction from other similar venues such as the beer garden. This study by McNamara fills these gaps and provides a foundation for even further investigation.

Don B. Wilmeth
Brown University

Preface

Why should anyone care about the life and death of the New York concert saloon? There are, I suppose, at least a few reasons that appear here, along with the details of operation. First, the concert saloon is a "new" form of American entertainment, relatively little known to the public or, for that matter, to scholars. As I point out, the concert-saloon show was apparently designed as a musical entertainment, but it contained other elements. It seems to have been influenced by the minstrel show, variety, and all the other American popular entertainments of the day, as well as by British music hall. In turn, it almost certainly influenced American vaudeville and early burlesque. But the New York concert saloon has hardly been written about – and certainly never in detail – and it often has been conflated with the variety theatre, which it resembled in many ways and to which it was related. But it was a unique and extraordinary form.

Perhaps it is quite enough that this book has provided new information about an origin of American vaudeville and burlesque. But, in addition, it suggests a few of the ways in which the concert saloon was operated and influenced by non-musical popular forms. Another point is that this book does for the concert saloon what I also attempted to do earlier for the medicine show in my book *Step Right Up* – to suggest that there is a link between entertainment and the growth of advertising in America after the Civil War. Increasingly, advertising seems to have used popular entertainment as a tool – and it obviously continues to do so today. In the nineteenth century, both the medicine show and the concert saloon seem, for example, to have been important, little-discussed parts of that development.

And finally – by implication, at least – this book is about the influence of entertainment in America. It reflects my long-held conviction that live popular entertainment is important, not perhaps because it was so good – much of it clearly was not – but because it is so much an expression of those who created it and watched it. Like radio and television in the twentieth century, one can scarcely talk about performance in the second half of the nineteenth century without bringing up the concert saloon. Not to do so would be to tell only part of the story of performance in America. Perhaps the nineteenth-century American theatre was not precisely what we thought it was. The details of the New York concert saloon suggest that conclusion.

In a way, this book is a detective story. There has always been a great deal of mystery about what constituted a nineteenth-century concert saloon. They have often been confused with variety houses, ordinary saloons, dance houses, and other establishments. And very little has been written about the shows that appeared there. Indeed, references to the concert saloon from the period – and later – *are* often misleading, and one may legitimately come to different conclusions about what was and was not a concert saloon and what took place there. But a few sources help when they are studied in detail, even though much remains to be done. This book employs two of those sources in relation to the New York concert saloon – the New York *Clipper* and some of the papers of The Society for the Prevention of Juvenile Delinquents. It also uses the works of James Mc Cabe and other commentors.

The *Clipper* was first published in 1853. Its editor at the time was Harrison Trent, and it was founded as a fairly conventional "sporting and theatrical" paper, covering, in addition to the theatre, such topics as prize fighting, baseball, and walking races. It was sold to Frank Queen in 1855. Between about 1865 and 1875, it was the only American newspaper carrying extensive news about popular performance forms such as minstrelsy, variety halls, circus, and concert saloons and their shows. In so doing, as William Slout points out, it became known as "The Showman's Bible." Competition from *Billboard* and *Variety* caused the paper to close in 1924.

Some years ago, I became aware of a series of fourteen *Clipper* articles from 1864, a great repository of material on the male-oriented concert saloon and its shows in New York. At the time of the so-called Concert Bill, two years earlier, the concert saloons had been widely discussed in the newspapers and other periodicals. But later they were profiled in a series in the *Clipper*, the only New York paper with a genuinely sustained interest in them.

As a publication widely read by nineteenth- and early twentieth-century showmen, the *Clipper* naturally portrayed concert saloons as relatively innocuous if somewhat colorful haunts. It *did* discuss them in detail, however. The *Clipper* series, which ran from January 2 through April 3, 1864, is known to some historians but much neglected. It provides a great deal of useful information, but it struck me at the time that there was not enough for a book.

Later, however, I was given a collection of reports on concert saloons and their shows, created by the Society for the Reformation of Juvenile Delinquents, dating from about 1874 to about 1884. The Society, a venerable organization, had for some time operated a famous reformatory, the House of Refuge. The Society, founded in the early nineteenth century, had become something of a New York City institution. It was a prominent and powerful organization in the City, and the legislature was anxious to tap into that prominence and power when they needed help. And, as we shall see, the Society was willing to cooperate.

I own about twenty-four boxes of Society materials. The various documents (many of which describe male-oriented New York concert saloons or their inmates) were designated to be used in the Supreme Court of the state of New York. A majority of these documents are in effect reports by investigators hired by the Society. (Of course, like the *Clipper* reporters, none of the investigators was a prominent New Yorker. They were simply ordinary men, hired to investigate – or, if the reader prefers, to spy on – concert saloons, and later other institutions.) The reports provide information about the operation of the concert saloons, as well as about changes that took place after the so-called Concert Bill was passed in April of 1862, and a later licensing bill was passed in 1872 and amended in 1875 and 1876. It struck me that the information in these reports, though not complete, when put together with the *Clipper* articles, offered good pictures of an almost unknown American post-Civil War theatrical institution, as well as its offerings.

My later Society reports, especially, provide information on German beer gardens, variety theatres, and other performance venues investigated by the Society, on the grounds that they *might* be concert saloons, even though they were called something else. The majority – not all – of the reports before about 1874 and after approximately 1884 are missing, probably discarded many years ago. Perhaps they will turn up at a later date. I hope so; there is much more to be done.

It soon became clear from both the *Clipper* articles and the Society reports that the New York concert saloons were influenced by minstrelsy, variety, and a kind of pre-burlesque burlesque, as well as other American popular forms, and, very likely British singing saloons, pleasure gardens, and of course the music hall. Much of the material makes clear these relationships. This book revolves around the *Clipper* articles and the Society papers. Some chapters depend primarily on one, some on another. In a few chapters I use both of them. My chief sources seem to hold very different points of view about the concert saloon. In fact, they do. The Society was rigidly proper, quite different from the live-and-let-live *Clipper*. But I have also used other works, as well.

An example is the work of James Mc Cabe, Jr. A prominent New York guidebook editor of the concert-saloon era, his guides are widely known, but take on a new importance in the light of the Society documents and the *Clipper* articles. Indeed, his views became an important addition because they are colorful and personal, if slightly hysterical. One sees the concert saloon more clearly through contemporary eyes because Mc Cabe wrote about it. The son of a minister, Mc Cabe (born Edward Winslow Martin) seems to have inherited much of his father's point of view about morality. In many ways he was superficially a reformer, though, like most writers of guides to the City, he was also commercially minded, and understood what his readers wanted. His pictures of the concert saloon and the other low-life haunts of New York are mixed in certain subtle ways. His ambivalence makes him a useful witness: He was aghast at the goings on in the concert saloons of the metropolis, but not *too* aghast to offer interesting texture.

From 1868 to 1882 Mc Cabe produced several guidebooks to the City. In all of them he provided a grim – but titillating – portrait of the concert saloon. I have used material about concert saloons and other cheap entertainment venues from his *Secrets of the Great City* (1868), *Lights and Shadows of New York Life* (1872), and *New York by Sunlight and Gaslight* (1882), re-issued as *New York by Gaslight*. In them Mc Cabe was quite specific about the dangers concert saloons presented – as well as their seedy allure. He seemed to be saying, "stay away from concert saloons. They are evil. But if you *do* go, you will encounter a kind of anonymity found only in New York."

Of course, I also employ other sources on the nineteenth century, including M. B. Leavitt's useful *Fifty Years in Theatrical Management, 1859–1909*, a number of newspaper and magazine articles, and a few other books. Occasionally there is some helpful more or less modern commentary, for example, material from Herbert Asbury's invaluable *The Gangs of New York*. But the chief sources are the Society papers and the *Clipper* articles.

To recap: the Concert Bill took place in 1862, and a second bill in 1872, which I give in full in Appendix I, with important additions taking place in 1875 and 1876. The *Clipper* articles appeared in the winter and spring of 1864. The Society papers range from about 1874 to about 1884, with scattered material earlier and later. My major sources, however, require some additional interpretation: the *Clipper* author (or authors, we do not know) writes in a slangy, often impenetrable "insider" style that reminds one of the later *Variety*. And, of course, the articles were written for an audience that already was generally familiar with concert saloons and, hence, leave out some important detail.

In general, the Society for the Prevention of Juvenile Delinquents reports use the phrase "concert room" interchangably with "concert saloon." In addition, the reports refer constantly to "minstrels" as appearing in concert saloons, by which they do not mean the blackface minstrels of the day. In fact, the reporters are simply using an archaic word that at the time corresponded roughly to "variety performers" or "variety artists" – singers, dancers, musicians, comedians, and the like – rather than so-called legitimate stage actors.

Blackface minstrels did indeed perform in many, if not all, concert saloons – in fact, they probably provided the bulk of material – but they were ordinarily referred to in the Society documents as "negro minstrels"; minstrel performances by actual *blacks* took place in some concert saloons, but the phrase "negro minstrels" seems usually to have referred to white men in blackface.

Women seem not to have blacked up on concert-saloon stages. Females did, however, often appear in concert saloons. Some of them were "waiter girls," and of course some were patrons, or dancers and singers in the show. Sometimes – perhaps in addition to their other duties as waiter girls or performers or both – women were "in-house" prostitutes. In fact, it is not clear what percentage of New York concert saloons had attached houses of prostitution. Some did; some did not. By the same token, it is unclear how many of the routines and songs performed on their stages were scatological. Some were; some were not.

With these caveats in mind, both the *Clipper* articles and the reports by Society investigators provide highly detailed information about what appeared there. I do not deal in detail with institutions not mentioned in the *Clipper* articles or the Society documents, with the exception of two forms related to the concert saloon that I cover late in the book – dance houses and German beer gardens.

Dance houses are usually not discussed by the Society for the Prevention of Juvenile Delinquents, since, although they were avowedly "low," they generally did not offer shows, and the Society was only genuinely interested – at least at first – in institutions that featured alcohol, shows, and – especially – the institution of the waiter girl. Most of the German beer gardens, many of them on the lower East Side of New York, were more or less respectable and catered to a reputable clientele, including wives and children of male patrons.

But the direction of the law changed, and with it the concerns of the Society. Some dance houses and German beer gardens were, in fact, investigated by the Society in the later years – almost certainly in part because of the Society's continued need for money, and in part because they were suspected of being concert saloons in disguise. The book also considers a few other forms that were given a hard look by the Society after the war, such as unauthorized theatrical performances in hired halls, small theatres, and the like. In fact, however, the old male-oriented concert saloon was dying out in New York in the seventies and early eighties, along with the institution of the waiter girl.

As much as possible, I have tried to work the necessary references into the text. I have been as complete as I can be in my references to particular concert saloons, including the address, if I know it, the first time a concert saloon is mentioned, as well as the year (sometimes the day and month) when information about it or its acts appears in a *Clipper* article or a Society report. I have only provided notes on lengthy direct quotations (if they are not already identified in the text). In addition, I have tried to explain in the text any names, places, or objects connected with the theatre that I imagined would not be familiar to most readers. At the end of the book I have provided a list of useful sources, some of which I have used here and some of which shed light on concert saloons or the forms of entertainment that influenced them or were influenced *by* them.

A number of examples were possible in the chapters, but in an attempt to avoid anything like an annals, I have selected only a few examples that relate directly to the theatrical (and, of course, musical) practice of New York concert saloons. In general, I have not changed spelling or grammar, or interpreted nineteenth-century slang, except when not to do so would have resulted in confusion. When I have made changes, they are generally silent.

I should also point out that my aim was to investigate certain entertainment topics concerned with the New York concert saloon rather than offering a comprehensive account of all the various changes that took place in the period 1864–1884. Here, I simply treat an unusual example of entertainment history.

Another item is worth mentioning: the book handles details of New York concert-saloon practice from the mid-1860s through the mid-1880s as though there were few significant changes in that period, except that the waiter girl fell out of fashion and "family" entertainment became more common in concert saloons and elsewhere. Perhaps there *were* other important changes that I have not caught, but the male-oriented concert saloon seems to have been basically traditional and "conservative" in its operation. Concert saloons disappeared with alarming frequency. But there do not appear to be many substantial alterations in the way surviving concert saloons operated until the fad for waiter girls declined and the family-oriented establishments became popular in the late seventies and eighties.

Of course, this book does not attempt to catalogue *all* the male-oriented concert saloons that existed in New York. There were many others. In that sense, then, the book is roughly the opposite of my earlier work, *Day of Jubilee*, published in 1998. In that book I attempted to pull together all of the chief celebrations of nineteenth-century New York, and to find the common theatrical devices; this book tries to analyze in detail a limited number of documents – and concert saloons – in a limited time span, primarily to reconstruct the details of operation of an important nineteenth-century New York entertainment institution. But both books have a somewhat similar purpose. In this book, as in *Day of Jubilee,* I attempt to draw attention to – to widen the public vision of – aspects of a popular performance form in New York.

The *Clipper* articles and a few other essays were collected in 1994 in book form as an anthology called *Broadway Beneath the Sidewalk,* carefully edited by William Slout. I have taken a number of things from his anthology and I owe Slout a great debt. A number of other works use a discussion of the concert saloon to introduce a different topic, often vaudeville or burlesque. Scholars who have dealt intelligently, but not at length, with the concert saloon include Robb Snyder, in his *Voice of the City,* an account of vaudeville as popular culture in New York, Robert C. Allen, in *Horrible Prettiness,* his history of burlesque, and Richard Butsch, in his recent *The Making of American Audiences.*

Edwin G. Burrows and Mike Wallace have included a very good, brief account of the concert saloon in *Gotham,* their history of New York to 1898. My old friend Parker Zellers, wrote a 1968 article in *Educational Theatre Journal,* "The Cradle of Variety : The Concert Saloon." So far as I know, it is one of the few modern articles – if not the only article – on the subject. I have used the Zellers piece in my book. It was especially helpful about the

earliest and latest concert saloons. Sometimes, however, I arrive at different
conclusions from his because I have new information. In addition, I have
been helped a great deal in my thinking by Madelon Powers' *Faces Along the
Bar*, an account of late nineteenth- and early twentieth-century working-
men's saloons. Marilyn Wood Hill's *Their Sisters' Keepers*, about prostitution
in New York City to 1870, and G. C. D. Odell's compendious *Annals of the
The New York Stage*, were also important to me. And of course I have learned
much about the world from which the concert saloon came from Herbert
Asbury's classic *The Gangs of New York*, and from the always useful *Police
Gazette*.

It might be of help to point out what is *not* intended. The music hall
in Britain was obviously important. But it is not discussed, except as one
influence on the New York concert saloon; the music hall is a complex subject and deserves its own treatments. Likewise, this book is not focused on
explaining the impact of the concert saloon on the society of Civil War and
post-Civil War New York, except as that connection is inevitable. Conversely, it does not try to deal in detail with the influence of that society on
the concert saloon, except where it also is inevitable. Such studies remain to
be done. This book is about a popular entertainment venue and what took
place there.

But I am glad to have provided some background on a virtually unknown
piece of American entertainment history. I trust that my book will sketch
out some details of a pivotal moment in the life of the concert saloon and will
awaken interest in and add to our knowledge of the popular entertainment
of New York City – and of entertainment in nineteenth-century America.

Brooks McNamara
New York City

Acknowledgments

I want to thank my wife Nan McNamara for her endless patience with my somewhat unusual topic, as well all those who also have assisted in some way in the preparation of these chapters. First among those to receive my heartfelt thanks of course are William Slout, editor of *Broadway Beneath the Sidewalk*, William Asadorian of the Queens Public Library, and Leo Hurwitz of Queens College of the City University for their kindness and thoughtfulness. I want to thank the irrepressible Parker Zellers for early incarnations of the idea. And for helpful advice throughout, I must also thank my friend Jim Hatch. Another friend, Don Wilmeth, also offered advice and gave me the opportunity to read a paper, which represents an origin of this book, at Brown University, and was especially helpful in editing it. I would also like to thank the faculty and staff of the University of Canterbury, Kent, where I read another paper about the concert saloon. Elements of both talks appear here in different forms.

Even an intentionally limited book spreads out in time and space. I appreciate the help of my assistant Sylvia Wang, and my former assistant Liz Cherubino-Hess. I also am grateful to my friend George Thompson of the Reference Room of the New York University Library, my daughter Jane McNamara, formerly of the New York Public Library, now of the Los Angeles Conservancy, Andy Davis and the staff of the Museum of the City of New York, and to the following institutions and their staffs: the Billy Rose Collection of the New York Public Library, the Hatch-Billops Collection, the Society for Prevention of Cruelty to Children, the Archives of the City of New York, the New York University Library, the New York University Law Library, the Special Collections at Brown University, and of course The Shubert Archive.

Prologue: sources of the concert saloon and its shows

The concert saloons are among the social evils. They flourish along certain parts of Broadway, Sixth Avenue and the Bowery, and are simply so many places where the devil's work is done. They provide a low order of music, and the service of the place is rendered by young women, many of whom are dressed in tights and all sorts of fantastic costumes, the chief object of which is to display the figure as much as possible.

James Mc Cabe, *New York by Sunlight and Gaslight*, 1882

WHAT WERE THE CONCERT SALOONS OF NEW YORK CITY? The answer is not too complex. Essentially, they were saloons that presented free or low-cost shows as a device to attract (chiefly male at first) customers. The shows featured music – but not, as we shall see, exclusively. They flourished in New York City during, and for twenty years or so after, the Civil War. Most were saloons refitted or initially equipped to include simple stages, probably without traps, flys (if they existed at all) that included only the most basic rigging, and one or two stock settings. A few were in former theatres, but the majority of concert saloons – not all – seem to have had a bar and a flat floor to accommodate tables and chairs for the drinkers/audience members. A few – nobody knows how many – also promoted gambling by their patrons.

Most – especially during the Civil War era – also had "waiter girls" who served drinks to male customers and sat with them, receiving tokens or tickets in exchange for drinks. But, although waiter girls were almost invariably identified as part-time prostitutes, some may have been simply bar maids and perhaps stage entertainers. Some concert saloons did have so-called "private boxes" or "private rooms," used to facilitate prostitution or assignation. But again, nobody knows how many; however, it is clear that

I

this was the beginning of the bad reputation that concert saloons carried from that time on.

So far as is known, concert saloons were not "tied" houses – to use the British term – that is, they were not owned by a particular brewery or distillery. Rather, they were independent, privately owned institutions. Often, but not always, owners and managers were the same people – mostly men, but occasionally women. The owners or managers frequently acted as masters of ceremonies for the shows that took place in concert saloons. But not invariably; sometimes they hired musicians or other professional performers as masters of ceremonies.

Basically, then, concert saloons were little more than saloons with various kinds of shows. But the mix of females, alcohol, and stage entertainment was thought by many people of the Civil War era and after to promote immorality, wherever some version of the combination existed. It was especially feared and hated in the concert saloons: the dangers of alcohol were well known, the shows were felt to be provocative, and of course all waiter girls were felt to be, if not out-and-out prostitutes, little better than prostitutes. Indeed – if an equation is possible – concert saloons were believed to be civic nuisances, much as many later citizens of New York have often viewed "topless" and nude bars, pornographic bookstores, and gay bath houses as affronts to the city and to particular neighborhoods. Critics often have not always known exactly what went on in such places – but the activity was bound to be illegal and offensive. Its very existence proved that. So it was with the nineteenth-century New York concert saloons.

The waiter girls disappeared after the War, but a kind of concert saloon existed in some form or other in New York from before the Civil War until perhaps almost World War I. That is a generous estimate, however; by the turn of the century most had already become history in New York City. "Ten years ago," writes a columnist in *Current Literature* in 1901, "there were numerous 'dives' where now the hard working fathers and families are struggling to make enough to bring up their children as becoming citizens of America." By 1901, he says, such "joints" as did exist were found only below Canal Street on the Bowery. And anybody who was robbed elsewhere on the Bowery had only himself to blame.

But old-fashioned – and tough – male-oriented concert saloons also existed elsewhere in the United States. (A brief account of their spread across the United States is given in the Epilogue, but the full story has yet to be written.) At any rate, an account of their growth and change in New York, 1864–1884, is traced in this book, based primarily on the sources outlined in the Preface. If the book is not a complete history of the concert saloon, it has the advantage of being the first full-length study of the operation and fare of a mysterious but once-important New York institution. And it suggests what may well have gone on across America in the late nineteenth century and the first years of the century that followed.

When did the first concert saloon appear in the City? The answer is not easy, and perhaps not really too important, in any case. Drinking establishments of various kinds, of course, went back to the beginnings of New York. A number of them undoubtedly featured music and other entertainments and sometimes prostitutes, as well as alcohol. But the real vogue for concert saloons (or "concert halls," or "concert rooms," or "music halls," or "dives" or "free and easys," or "the shades," as they sometimes were called) came in the years surrounding the Civil War. In *Horrible Prettiness*, Robert C. Allen says that concert saloons were first mentioned in newspapers in 1850. Slout gives the date at which they "were sharing a sizable part of Broadway night life" as 1860. Both authors are probably more or less right. But it is undoubtedly safe to say simply that concert saloons first became popular in the City in the years before the Civil War, increased in popularity during the war, and altered as the century advanced. The first concert saloons in America may well have been in New York City. Or Philadelphia. No one knows. They may have been American versions of the British music hall. Again, no one knows.

It *is* known that there were perhaps half a dozen influences on concert saloons over the years. The center was, of course music – all concert saloons featured songs, and a large number provided purely instrumental music as well. Almost certainly an important influence was the British music hall, a source of popular song – and other variety acts – aimed at a chiefly working-class audience. The British music hall certainly resembled the American concert saloon in many important ways. Perhaps the French "cafe concert" or "cafe chantant" was also an influence, though that relationship is not very clear. In any case, there is a similarity. An outgrowth of the musical taverns that grew up in Paris in the eighteenth century, by the middle of the nineteenth century there were more than two hundred in Paris alone and many throughout France. They were purveyors of food and drink and various kinds of variety entertainment. At any rate, the January 1862 article in the New York *Post* thought that there was some relationship between the cafes chantants and the New York concert saloon. The writer says: "From the days of the 'Dog and Duck' and 'Finish,' London has had her night houses; Paris, whether monarchical, republican or Imperial, rejoices in her

WILTON'S NEW MUSIC HALL, WELLCLOSE SQUARE.

1 Wilton's Music Hall, Wellclose Square, London, n.d.

cafes chantants; and for the last two years, our cosmopolitan city of New York, emulous alike in good and evil, has produced as vicious and popular a perversion of the two as can be imagined."[1]

At any rate, beginning in the middle of the nineteenth century, the music hall, which had developed out of tavern shows and "Song and Supper" rooms, became a major part of British entertainment, especially for the working classes, although it was also frequented by representatives of every social level. The passage of the Theatres Registry Act of 1843 had confronted the owners of licensed premises with a hard choice. They could run a legitimate playhouse without refreshments, or they could operate a music hall in which drinks and food could be served but only variety entertainment could be presented. Many took the second option. By 1868, there were some twenty-eight music halls of all classes – from cheap and dismal to lavish – in London alone, and some 300 scattered around England. The show often featured a "compere" or master of ceremonies and various variety turns. They were considered cheap entertainment and "fast" by many conservative people.

The form was certainly familiar to American tourists traveling in Britain. And it was a haven for performers who worked outside the regular British theatres – in particular the Irish, who often emigrated to America, as minstrel performers and in other areas of theatre, bringing with them their songs and sketches and their knowledge of music-hall spaces.

But some concert saloons also featured an early form of burlesque and passed along to later American entrepreneurs many conventions and ways of doing business. The concert saloon also is referred to as a variant form of variety theatre and thus as an ancestor of vaudeville. From one point of view, it obviously was. But basically concert saloons were unique institutions – a kind of early musical theatre – although their shows also contained other kinds of variety entertainment. From variety, indeed, concert saloons borrowed a number of acts, many of which had already come from other sources. A number of acts which appeared on the concert-saloon stage of course also were seen in the variety theatres of the day. But most had originated in other forms of American popular entertainment. Performers in minstrelsy, dime museums, pleasure gardens, and the circus had gravitated to variety – and often to concert saloons, as well. But the concert saloon also has been seen as an ancestor of the night club. "The night clubs and cabarets that are such prominent features of our hectic night life," said *Valentine's Manual* in 1927, "are in the main euphemistic terms for what the Elegant Eighties knew as 'dives'."

In the July 23, 2001 *New Yorker*, Adam Gopnik points out that there is a modern institution, the "New Burlesque." "In the New Burlesque," he says, "the money is sort of incidental; the performers are into making art." In the *old* burlesque money was *not* incidental, however. It was the point. And the form that was to become full-blown burlesque was undoubtedly one of the most important influences on the concert saloon beyond music, because it brought in patrons, and hence money. In fact, an early incarnation of burlesque was one of the standard features of many New York concert saloons, and probably helped to lead to their bad reputations. In turn, concert saloon acts – and the ambiance of the concert saloons themselves – almost certainly influenced the course of early burlesque.

Originally, burlesques had been travesties or parodies of plays, operas, or important political or social events. In part, they were to become one of the elements in such musical extravaganzas as *The Black Crook* in 1866, and its sequel *The White Fawn* in 1868. *The Black Crook* was a sensation. From that point on, a host of imitations of every sort featured scantily clad chorus girls and the combination was increasingly appealing – and increasingly inoffensive – to large segments of the public.

In 1868 these influences also were combined with considerable success in *Ixion*, the first American production by the popular British Blondes, an

English troupe that appeared in the United States. They wore what were, for the time, extremely abbreviated costumes, and in the 1870s the vogue for British Blondes-style entertainments increased throughout America. Several imitation troupes appeared, at least one of which played concert saloons. Probably a number did, but we are given no clue in any of the sources, except that the moralists found the costumes of women on stage in concert saloons shocking in the extreme.

Manager M. B. Leavitt gave burlesque its essential form during the latter part of the nineteenth century. It featured chorus girls in revealing costumes, as well as some suggestive material. We know that Leavitt took part of his entertainment from the minstrel show. But the whole affair also must have owed a certain debt to the goings-on in concert saloons, where an ancestor of burlesque had been presented on a much smaller scale, and without the definition it was to achieve later. As Mc Cabe suggests, leg-show acts in concert saloons featured young women in scanty costumes, as well as music, jokes, and songs that were sometimes titillating – if not downright prurient – staples of later burlesque.

Minstrelsy – either directly or from the variety stage – was another major influence on concert saloons, and minstrel songs were among its staples. But it provided concert saloons with much more material than simply songs; minstrel quips, sketches, monologues, and much more, also appeared there. Minstrelsy was an American institution that had taken the country by storm at the middle of the nineteenth century. The white actor in blackface had appeared shortly after the first quarter of the century and had reached new heights of popularity with audiences in 1830, in the act by T. D. Rice, who performed a parody of a black stable hand in his famous and much imitated "Jim Crow" routine. The beginnings of minstrelsy as it was later to develop, however, came in 1843, when Dan Emmett and three other minstrels began to perform as "The Virginia Minstrels."

As it blossomed in the years leading up to the Civil War, many minstrel shows were divided into three "parts," the first of which featured white male performers in blackface (women did not ordinarily perform until very late in the history of minstrelsy), seated in a semi-circle, with the master of ceremonies or Interlocutor in the center, and Tambo and Bones, percussionists and comedians, at either end. In this part the performers sang songs, danced, played banjos and fiddles, and responded to jokes between the Interlocutor and the endmen. The second part was an "olio," a performance in front of the main curtain or drop, of sentimental songs, dances, and humorous monologues called "stump speeches." The third "part" was a "plantation afterpiece," or, in later years, some sort of parody of a popular book or play, or of an awkward political situation. Sometimes the parody was musical.

After the Civil War the emphasis was less on crude satires of the black man and increasingly at the expense of such emerging ethnic groups in America as the Irish, and the "Dutch," as the Germans were popularly called. In addition, a number of minstrel companies featuring actual blacks were organized after the war and gave the white men in blackface serious competition. By 1900, audiences were less interested and the so-called professional "Minstrel Craze" had begun to dissipate everywhere in America in a very serious way.

In 1911, Leavitt tried to set down some of the reasons for the decline of minstrelsy in his autobiography, *Fifty Years in Theatrical Management*. "It is doubtful," he says, "if minstrelsy will ever be seen in its early existence, which at one time was the most popular form of amusement," because,

> The elaborate and spectacular manner that many managers have lately adopted to revive old-fashioned minstrelsy has gone wide of the mark, notwithstanding many of the old-time favorites are still in the field . . . The growth and success of vaudeville are other potent reasons for its decline. The extra-ordinary salaries offered have lured the other shining lights of the minstrel stage into the ranks of vaudeville, comic opera and musical comedy, where they obtain greater scope for versatility and increased remuneration. The public naturally followed its favorites and the minstrel patronage became greatly reduced, and it is now probably at a lower ebb of popularly and financially than ever before in its history.[2]

Newer forms, including the movies, had caught the fancy of popular audiences and absorbed much of the material previously presented in the minstrel show. But the hard times had already begun long before.

When the first minstrel men began to appear in large numbers in New York City, some of them almost certainly found that performing in such places as a variety theatre, a dime museum, a circus, a pleasure garden – or a concert saloon – was a necessary financial alternative when business was slow in minstrel halls. A major difference was that, in such places as the concert saloon, minstrel men presented their material as part of a bill of unrelated acts rather than as part of a show tied together by blackface and by an overarching theme built around fantasies about plantation life in the South. In other words, in the concert saloon, as in variety, a traditional minstrel turn was no longer part of a whole evening of similar acts and songs.

While a song – or joke or sketch, say – maintained a familiar association with minstrelsy, in the concert saloon it was being done in connection with many different kinds of popular material.

Concert saloons also probably shared personnel and material with the dime museums that were so common on the Bowery and in other entertainment areas. Some of the same talent and the same acts (generally edited where necessary for a family audience) were to be found in typical dime museum "lecture halls" – an invented name for the playhouses that existed in such buildings. If there were two versions, performers in both knew both. Like the concert saloon, the dime museum was an important popular venue that employed familiar songs, jokes, and sketches.

Circuses were still another influence. Circus is one of the oldest forms of popular entertainment in America. A small traveling circus was a feature of the early eighteenth century, and circus "amphitheatres" appeared before 1800 in many American towns. To supplement their regular equestrian numbers, managers added variety acts to their bills. During the nineteenth century the population growth in rural areas led to an increase in touring, and circus tents appeared by 1830. In the forties bands were featured, as well as bareback riding and similar thrilling feats. The development of railroads led to the movement of performers and animals by rail and, in large part, the replacement of the traditional wagon show. The circus now expanded tremendously.

In the 1850s, museum magnate P. T. Barnum had entered the circus business, later going into partnership with James Bailey, and helping to build the ante-bellum circus into an imaginative display that combined bareback riders, clowns, acrobats, freaks and animals. This idea, centered around a spectacular but essentially eclectic collection of entertainments, was later taken up by such figures as the Sells Brothers, who eventually were to merge their show with the old Barnum and Bailey circus. Many circus acts – and circus performers – eventually found their way onto the concert-saloon stage. It was a natural move. (Tony Pastor was perhaps the most famous of the New York entertainers and entrepreneurs to have got his start in circus.)

It is clear that many people who appeared at concert saloons also performed from time to time at pleasure gardens. Pleasure gardens existed in both Britain and America. Throughout the eighteenth century the gardens were found in London and other large cities in Great Britain and elsewhere, often as adjuncts to inns and taverns. They usually provided food, gambling, and various kinds of variety entertainment. Pleasure gardens first became popular in New York early in the nineteenth century, in part growing out of picnic groves, and serving as one ancestor of the later amusement park. In an era before the advent of the public park, these proprietary parks served as important sources of summer amusement, usually featuring fireworks, and amusement rides, as well as a number of performers, who often routinely appeared in other forms of popular entertainment, among them the concert saloon.

A final influence was probably the growth of advertising in the last quarter of the nineteenth century. At base, a show presented in a saloon was an effective advertising device, a kind of precursor of the sponsored entertainment that was to appear on American radio and television in later years. It was also the equivalent of "dragging the town," the parade at which advertising fliers were distributed by a circus or minstrel company. Perhaps the most obvious parallel was with the medicine show, which also developed in America in the Civil War period. Here various nostrums were pitched and the show represented the free or low-cost "come on" that brought potential buyers to the medicine-show lot. So it was with the concert saloons: alcohol – and apparently sometimes prostitution – constituted the chief attractions, and the performance, like the waiter girls, was the equivalent of the advertising parade. Unlike variety theatres, concert saloons sold drinks – and maybe more – as their main business, and the acts were basically the come-on, rather than the central attraction.

The show at the New York concert saloon during the Civil War and the decades following it was an eclectic form, depending heavily on song, but borrowing from virtually all of the successful types of American popular entertainment – and not limiting itself to American forms. These it combined with the saloon, the fad of the waiter girl (at first), and, in some cases, the house of prostitution, creating a sometimes rough-and-ready, sometimes elaborate kind of theatre. It is often confused with variety. It was clearly related to the British music hall in important ways, but it was not simply the music hall transported across the Atlantic; it seems to have been a distinctly American take on a kind of people's entertainment.

Many of the acts and songs seen in concert saloons during and after the war descended to early vaudeville and burlesque. In the case of burlesque, owners and managers institutionalized the sexual essence of the old male-oriented concert saloon – and in the process helped to limit their business.

Especially after the Civil War, some owners and managers, however, went the other direction, taking some pains to make their shows respectable enough for women and children. But "moral reform" was probably less on the minds of concert-saloon people than it was with some vaudeville entrepreneurs later. The realization that family entertainment represented an untapped resource, however, had almost certainly been a key issue. It almost certainly meant bigger audience potential – and hence assured survival. But in exploiting and systematizing suitable family entertainment, of course, they helped spell the death of the old male-oriented shows, probably without changing their character too much. There seems not to have been all that much to change. Yet, until its demise, the concert saloon was always surrounded by rumors – justified or not – of dark doings.

I

Where the devil's work is done: New York City concert saloons during the Civil War era

Well, it won't set you back a peg to visit this institution, for it is one of the attractions of the great metropolis.

The *Clipper* on the Canterbury, 1861

NEW YORK DURING THE CIVIL WAR WAS AMERICA'S LEADING commercial city and, according to the reformers and like-minded people, just what the majority of Americans thought – a sink of depravity. In 1866 a Methodist bishop named Matthew Simpson, for example, just after the war, estimated that New York City, which had about 800,000 citizens, harbored nearly 30,000 thieves, 20,000 prostitutes, 3,000 drinking establishments, and some 2,000 gambling dens. It did not matter whether Simpson's estimate was exaggerated, the fact remains that, during and after the Civil War, there was considerable illegal activity in New York City, and that great wealth, much of which was gained through dubious means, co-existed with grinding poverty. Of course there were both reformers and those who encouraged illegal activities such as the brothels, the gambling houses – and of course the concert saloons.

The concert saloons were of every sort, from the most humble to the most lavish. An article in the New York *Post* on January 2, 1862, trading on the publicity surrounding the up-coming Concert Bill, spoke of one elaborate concert saloon, the Canterbury, between Houston and Prince Streets, in what is now SoHo. It was in the building once occupied by the French Theatre, and was "the most prestigious on our list." The *Post* especially noted its large size and splendid mirrors. The article compared the grander concert saloons like the Canterbury to the Novelty, 616 Broadway, "a second-rate and comparatively smaller institution." But everything between them – and *below* the Novelty in quality – existed somewhere in the city, although the Bowery was probably their center.

At the time of the Civil War, the stage in all its forms had a bad reputation with many in New York, especially with some clergy and other conservative people. They saw only lurid displays of the female form in such popular mid-nineteenth century plays as *The Black Crook*, and in the controversial actress Adah Isaacs Menken's *Mazeppa*, as well as in the appearance in the city of the notoriously scantily clad act, The British Blondes.

Houses of prostitution – and the prostitutes themselves – of course, were viewed by reputable New Yorkers as a shocking social evil, especially with so many military men in the City. In addition, there had also been a groundswell for temperance among many respectable residents of the City, and, in some cases, for total abstinence. As a result, saloons – which already had bad reputations – had begun to be increasingly looked on askance by many. The fact that the concert saloons featured a kind of particularly tawdry, low-end theatre as well as liquor and the new fad of "waiter girls" – and, in the minds of many, prostitution – was too much for many so-called respectable people to bear. As late as 1881, *Nym Crinkle* would point out, "they serve as the gathering places for idle and vicious people to drink beer, listen to execrable music, make assignations, and parade in the dirtiest market those common charms which they have to sell." Their reputations continued to be bad as long as they existed.

But that was not all. Another important factor was the reputation of the Bowery and lower Broadway as "fast." The Bowery was then a cheap entertainment area that ran – and runs today – roughly from Chatham Square, below Houston Street, to Cooper Union, some fourteen blocks north. About the street, a modern history by Lloyd Morris, *Incredible New York*, says that, in the middle of the nineteenth century, "On Saturday and Sunday nights, the Bowery was in full carnival. Along its whole length, the avenue blazed with light, rang with the music of German street bands, Italian organ grinders, itinerant harpists and violinists, the cries of street vendors, the shouts of barkers who strove to lure the passing throng into the shops."[1] And of course there were the concert saloons that lined the street, along with billiard parlors, dime museums, and houses of prostitution. There were still concert saloons – and the houses of prostitution associated in the public mind with them – on the Bowery in 1892 when Charles Hoyt and Percy Gaunt wrote about the street in a famous and much quoted song, "The Bowery," in Hoyt's play *A Trip To Chinatown*. By then the street was becoming less an entertainment district and more a haven for the unemployed and for chronic alcoholics. But to many, more than ever, the infamous Bowery – and with it the concert saloon – still offered a taste of "one of the devil's own nights."

2 "Saturday Night on the Bowery," woodcut, c. 1875

Even before the Civil War, the Bowery had been consistently spoken of by reformers as a sinister place, the resort of "toughs" and gang members. Some time after 1870 it was on the way to becoming a genuine "skid row." By 1882, toward the end of the period discussed in this book, a report by the Bowery Mission and Home for Young Men called the street "the centre of one of Satan's strongholds." The report continued, adding that "haunts of vice and crime line [the street] which is nightly thronged with a mingled multitude of thoughtless youth, hardened criminals, and neglecters of all places of wholesome, and especially Christian influence." The mission estimated that at the beginning of the eighties some "15,000 persons, mostly young men – nightly throng its places of amusement." Not the least of the places were the concert saloons.

Although a great many concert saloons of the war years seem to have been in or near the Bowery, some of the better ones (or at least the more lavish) were in lower Broadway, above Houston Street, along with a jumble of other tourist institutions. Broadway was generally a number of cuts above the Bowery as far as its outward appearance was concerned. But there was something not altogether respectable about it. The street was an extraordinarily varied one, housing some of the finest shops in the city and some

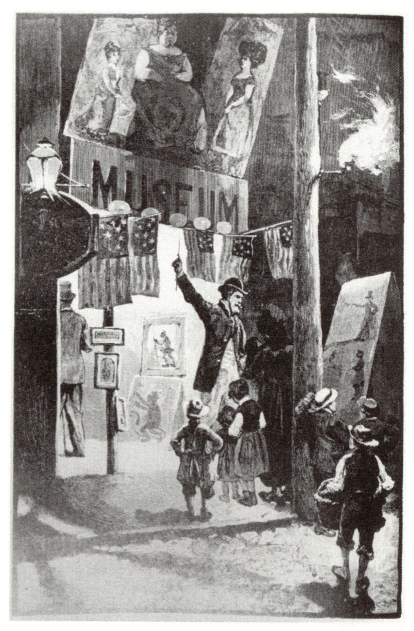

3 Outside "talker" at a dime museum, Harry Muhrman, *Harper's Weekly*, February 26, 1881

fairly raucous saloons of one sort or another. An 1878 article in *Harper's New Monthly Magazine* begins by acknowledging this fact, which had been true for years. "Life on Broadway is pretty nearly everything. It is the broadest farce, the heaviest tragedy, and the most delicate comedy; it is tender, severe, sad, and joyous – an available text for the satirist, the moralist, the humorist, the preacher, and the man of the world. No ambition, passion, or creed may not be studied in its magnificent parade, which puts together things that by nature are widely apart, a grand ensemble of vividly dramatic contrasts."[2]

If the Bowery and the area around it (Green Street, for example, and Mercer Street) seem to have been the center of at least the low end of concert-saloon activity, and lower Broadway of some of the better establishments, a number of them were also to be found in other areas of the city. Thus, some concert saloons were to be located in another "tough" area, Hell's Kitchen, (now called "Clinton" and bounded roughly by Forty-second and Fifty-ninth Street, Eighth Avenue and the Hudson River), in Sixth Avenue, in the so-called Tenderloin (roughly from Thirty-fourth Street to Forty-second Street, between Fifth and Seventh Avenue). During the period discussed in this book, concert saloons were also seen on streets near the Bowery. Houston Street, which intersects the Bowery, seems to have been a favorite, and was the site of the famous Harry Hill's, which is discussed later.

Obviously, a major source of the concert-saloon show between 1864 and 1884 was the tradition of the concert-saloon show itself as it had existed before the Civil War. In volume six of Odell's famous *Annals of the New York Stage*, he reports a flourishing concert-saloon industry in New York in 1857, presenting music of various kinds and a wide range of other entertainments. He notes two dozen concert saloons in his "miscellany" section and tells us, for example, that on January 3, 1857, *The Herald* announced about the Bowery Concert Hall, 257 Bowery, later the Melodeon, that it offered "Music for the Million" and "Free Concerts Every Evening," and advised tourists not to leave the city without visiting this popular place. But the entertainment was not just musical; in addition to comic and ballad singers and several dancers (including a jig dancer), the author lists two comedians and an "Ethiopian delineator" who appeared in the show.

At the grandest concert saloons like the Canterbury, at any rate, it is clear that, before the passage of the Concert Bill, the entertainments were not confined solely to music – and usually with free or low-cost admission. On the eve of the Concert Bill, which shut down a number of shows, the Canterbury produced entertainments that were very large, sometimes made up of more than thirty acts. In 1860, in addition to a broad selection of musical acts, one could see a team of gymnasts, a tableau, cannon ball juggling, something called "The Flower Girl's Festival," and feats with a twenty-five-pound globe. An article in the *Clipper* in 1861, about an evening in the Canterbury, mentions, as well as music, such acts as a pole exercise, ladder groupings, acrobatic feats, a pantomime, a dramatic sketch, dances, a leap from a swinging rope into the auditorium, and an appearance "by a live Indian – Oka-ta-Walla." In the first paragraph the article attests to the popularity of the Canterbury in the year before the Concert Bill: "We spent a rainy evening there last week and eleven o'clock caught us before we were aware we had been an hour in the place. Time takes to itself wings and speeds away with lightning-like rapidity when the company is pleasant, so it is said; and so we found it on the occasion of our visit . . ."

The piece ends, significantly, with these words: "This . . . will give the readers an idea of what may be seen for a mere trifle at a New York concert saloon, the price of admission to the Canterbury being thirteen, twenty-five and thirty-five cents. The house is nightly crowded in every part, and our little 'waiter girl' is kept busy in supplying the wants of her numerous admirers."

But the potential onset of the Civil War had brought problems for the theatre. As M. B. Leavitt, the burlesque entrepreneur, put it in his autobiography, "The year 1860 made great changes in theatrical affairs, when the election of the first Republican President – Abraham Lincoln – threatened immediate dissolution of the Union. Business was paralyzed for a time and the theatre suffered severely." Many theatres changed hands, he says, while minstrel houses "were in turn severely crippled by the prevailing financial distress. The music halls [concert saloons] suffered least." In the first year of the Civil War all was well with the theatres again. Then the slump came, and managers "literally grabbed farmer boys from the streets," offering them "inducements to go on the stage and act." Something had to be done by the theatre and minstrel managers. And shortly it was. The result was the Concert Bill.

The bill was possible because *all* of the concert saloons in New York City had a bad name. As Mc Cabe suggests in the quotation that begins the Prologue, they were associated in the public mind with drunkenness, bawdy entertainment, prostitution, and worse. As Leavitt and others point out, more established branches of the theatre, as well as the minstrel show, resented concert saloons because they were taking away badly needed audience members. As Leavitt says, things got even worse for the theatres and minstrel halls and better for concert saloons:

> Among the earliest to feel the return of better times were [the concert saloons]. These had become extremely numerous, perhaps because of the increasing number of soldiers. In making their appeal to the public they placed the greatest stress on announcing the "pretty waitresses" they employed. A wave of protest against them was started. The managers of the principal play-houses alleged that the vending of liquor by females was surely killing legitimate attractions. Many ministers of the Gospel preached sermons on the subject and in a short time an Act was passed forbidding women from serving drinks in any place of amusement.[3]

By 1861, theatre owners and managers, who resented the competition of the concert saloons, had begun to issue petitions aimed at suppressing them.

There was probably another important contributing reason, too. Certainly, the social position of the actor was not high in the years surrounding the war, and that of the popular entertainer was even lower; as a group, they were poor and uneducated, as well as being involved in a supposedly godless professsion. And those who performed in concert saloons were the lowest of the low. In particular, concert-saloon entertainers were easily connected with the criminal and the immoral in the minds of many right-thinking people. Public opinion was wholeheartedly against them.

Popular performers, then, were already tainted, and the places where they entertained – which obviously catered to all sorts of nameless horrors – hardly helped their image. Thus, any kind of performers in concert saloons were essentially defenseless against charges of immorality, even when their acts were fairly innocuous – as many appear to have been. But by definition, they *had* to be doing something wrong if they were performing in concert saloons; the combination of alcohol, waiter girls, presumed prostitution, and supposedly bawdy theatrical entertainment was simply too much for many middle-class people to stomach. Not that the entertainers did not sing songs and present comedy that was suggestive, or even obscene. They did. But the reports suggest concert saloons did not produce – and entertainers did not present – nearly as much "blue" material as reformers seemed to indicate. In fact, most acts of all kinds were probably basically innocuous, except to the most puritanical of critics.

At any rate, there was certainly confusion in the weeks before the Concert Bill. And a touch of hope. The saloon owners thought their lawyers could stave off the worst. Concert saloon supporters predicted, wrote the New York *Times* on April 26, 1862, that the courts "will have decided that since liquor-selling, theatrical performances and pretty waiter girls are separately legal and proper, that when they are conjoined they cannot be prohibited by any constitutional statute." It was wrong. Eventually, the owners and managers got the ear of the politicians in Albany, who used the presence of "waiter girls," in combination with alcohol and shows, as the very reason for their legislation.

But morality probably was not the crucial issue for the theatres – it seemingly was an excuse to force out of business unwanted competition. The bill seemed to be aimed in large part at the rapidly proliferating concert saloons, which theatre owners and managers thought were unfairly competitive. In any case, in January of 1862, a senator named Robins introduced a bill in the state legislature "to preserve the peace and order in public places in the City of New York." The initial justification of the bill was that it made it more difficult to pollute the morals – with alcohol and waiter girls, and shows – of Union soldiers and sailors stationed in or near the City – and of course of others, including juveniles.

Essentially, the Concert Bill made it unlawful to conduct any kind of spoken or sung "performance" in the entertainment venues of New York – "interludes, tragedies, comedies, operas, ballets, plays, farces, minstrelsy, or any other stage entertainment" – until a license had been obtained from the City. (And what constituted a performance was not clear.) In any case, no license was to be given to any place where wine, beer, or ardent spirits were sold when female "waiter girls" – who clearly "hustled" drinks and of course were widely suspected of being prostitutes, as well – were permitted to be present. The fine for infractions was then a large one, as much as $500, along with six months imprisonment.

The new bill went into effect on April 24, 1862, and – theoretically, at least – did produce the desired results, although, as Wilkes' *Spirit of the Times* suggested in May of 1864, "the keepers of such places have sufficient influence with the bench and the bar to evade or deny the execution of any law designed to restrain their devilish business." But many concert saloons turned out not to have "sufficient influence" and went out of business. Others stopped serving liquor, or giving shows, or fired their waiter girls. In any case, after the Concert Bill was passed in 1862, the overall size of the average show now seems to have shrunk and sometimes featured scarcely half the number of acts presented before the war years. At the less important institutions the number of acts often seems to have been even smaller. And non-musical acts were now becoming scarce in *any* concert saloons.

The Concert Bill was hard to interpret, and many owners and managers were being careful. It was widely thought that musical acts of any kind – since they were not really "shows" or "performances" – were exempt from the

Concert Bill, and for a while at least many concert saloons apparently tested out the theory by presenting material that they claimed was exclusively musical. It was worth a try, at any rate. Some attempted to get around the law by having only a piano or fiddle on the premises, or by sponsoring a kind of "community sing" among their customers, which had the double advantage of being both cheap and – at first glance – legal under the Concert Bill.

Others, however, stayed very much in the traditional business, giving what were obviously illegal shows free or for a small charge to customers – that is, retaining some combination of shows, alcohol, and their waiter girls, and trusting to luck that their activities would not be discovered. In 1862, for example, there still were probably in excess of seventy traditional concert saloons of all kinds operating illegally in New York – which is to say, in Manhattan, since consolidation was more than thirty years in the future. But most paid at least surface attention to the Concert Bill, although it was confusing. It was difficult, almost impossible to determine what was legal and what was not, but the legislators and some officials of the City of New York liked it that way.

It worked – at least to a certain extent. In volume seven of his *Annals*, Odell wrote about the coming of the Concert Bill and its immediate aftermath, pointing out that "all this froth and frivolity of drink and variety ran, we remember, synchronously with the darkest days of the Civil War, when we might suppose people were on their knees praying for peace on earth and a life free from heartbreaking worry!" He continued, quoting from the *Herald*:

> The legislature at Albany [had] passed a law against such resorts, and the New York police at once stopped the sale of liquor by the "waitresses" so much advertised by places like the Gaieties, and especially flaunted in a publication advertised in the Herald of April 6th: Belles of the Concert Saloon . . . a complete list of the Waiter Girls of New York, with a portrait and biography of each – "one hundred engravings and three hundred pages." On April 26th the Herald stated that the 'Broadway [and Bowery, etc.] concert saloons, with one or two exceptions, complied with the law last night, and in all probability, this week will end all of them.

Odell went on, quoting from the *Herald*. The police, it said, kept a close watch on each concert saloon found to be open:

> Canterbury Hall was well attended, Fox, the proprietor was complying with the law, "by closing his bar and allowing no females among the

audience." At the Melodeon, however, a number of girls were in attendance, but withdrawn by the command of Captain Helms, "though they
intend to continue them every night as they do not wait on the gentlemen." The Gaieties opened, with only theatrical performances.[4]

The concert saloon probably was, in large part, a political target, and the
new bill understandably was not a popular one with either liberal spirits or
concert saloon promoters. Many people, indeed, thought that the Concert
Bill was confusing, clumsy, and unfair. "Why," asked the *Mirror*, "this in-
vidious selection of [popular entertainment] for the payment of a penalty
which aligns it with the criminal classes and the violators of social order?"
Slout quotes a *Clipper* editorial written at the time, pointing to the obvious
lack of evenhandedness behind the Bill:

> Are the theatres altogether free from the drinking business? We think not.
> Attached to nearly, if not quite every theatre in this city, is a bar-room or
> more properly speaking a "drinking station." Entrances to these saloons
> are, in some instances, actually connected with the auditorium, check
> takers being stationed at such entrances to pass and repass those who
> may be desirous of taking their "beverage" . . . Indeed, in one or two of
> our theatres we have seen liquor brought into the auditorium and handed
> to purchasers in their seats.[5]

Many theatres, said the *Clipper*, were themselves unsavory establishments, whether alcohol was served or not, and whether or not the infamous
waiter girls were present: "The charge of immorality brought against concert saloons," the paper said, "might also, to a certain extent, be brought
against our theatres, for many of the 'pretty ballet girls' that are made to do
duty in low necked dresses and short skirts at theatres at so much per night
are no better in a moral point of view than some of those 'pretty waiter girls'
we are accustomed to see at music halls."

It was also clear that one result of the 1862 bill was not precisely what
prominent theatre owners expected – though, from some points of view,
what they deserved. "In making the attempt," said the New York *Times*,
"they have bitten themselves." As the newspaper pointed out, the bill had
backfired on some of its originators. First, and most obviously, "not alone
are the concert saloons amenable to the new law, but the theatres are alike
sufferers, for on Thursday evening the bar rooms connected with Niblo's
Garden, Wallack's, the Winter Garden, etc., were closed according to the
law, and thus some of the very men who set the ball in motion are first to feel
its 'depressing effect'." The ultimate reason was that "many of the theatrical

drinking saloons bring the managers large yearly sums of rent, and this sum cut off, they will atone in sackcloth and ashes for the part they took in the dirty work of attempting to kill off minor rival establishments."

In any case, the *Clipper* proceeded to make fun of the Concert Bill. In its 1864 series of articles, in a piece on the Oriental, it said: "When, in the spirit of mock morality, the gentlemen from the rural districts, represented at Albany, undertook to make laws for the Empire City, every sensible man laughed and snapped his fingers and thumb at their astute and asinine wisdom; but they were a 'power', and made themselves felt in many instances, particularly in abolishing waiter girls from concert halls." Anger at the upstate legislators (no unusual thing among Manhattanites) led to a fit of reminiscence on the reporter's part:

> Who of our young fellows doesn't look back with pleasure to the time when Fox's Canterbury and Rivers' Melodeon were in full blast, when on dull Sunday evenings a person could go and sip sherry cobblers and mint juleps – served up by delicate, lily white hands, belonging to young girls with alabaster "low necks," and silks and satins, short at both ends – and listen to a fine song and operatic instrumental music. Those were indeed "merry days of old," and formed one of the peculiar institutions of this great and glorious country.

At the end, the reporter returned to an indictment of legislators' veniality and hypocrisy, which, he felt, had caused much of the trouble in the first place:

> But it is a trite saying that "every dog has his day," and that with the theatrical combination and money shelled out to crush the waiter girl system, thinking that the concert saloon business would be knocked in the head at the same time, a law was eventually passed to abolish the good old custom, to the intense mortification and regret of both young and old bloods. We all know that these same legislators, who – goaded by that same power behind every throne, glittering gold, which was never known to fail – were instrumental in framing the obnoxious law, were the first to feel the effects of it when, away from home and family, they came down to York on "business," and missed their favorite crinolined divinities at the accustomed posts.[6]

The *Clipper*'s fourteen articles on the concert saloon provide an interesting picture of an entertainment that flourished during the Civil War. And it seems true, as it said, that concert saloons were immensely popular, both with soldiers and civilians, during the war years. But the catspaw, of course,

had been the Society for the Reformation of Juvenile Delinquents. As Alan
Neilsen says in *The Great Victorian Sacrilege*, it was one of a group of organizations that wielded considerable power in local affairs in the Civil War
era. The Society for the Reformation of Juvenile Delinquents and similar
"vice societies," were "funded by the wealthy," he says, "ostensibly for the
purpose of 'protecting' public morals. Many of these societies were all too
often a means of keeping [the public] under control. Although unallied
to any specific sect, they sought to promote Christian morality – in the
arts, as in society at large – through individual self-censorship and public
conformity."[7]

In 1839, a bill authorizing certain benefits for the Society for the Reformation of Juvenile Delinquents had already appeared before the New
York State Legislature. Its existence is specified in a set of papers that sur-
vive concerning an establishment called Hartmann's Theatre, 174 Forsyth
Street, in 1857. The papers say that Hartman has no license to present theatre
and continues that, after the fact, he and his employees are "restrained and
enjoined" from opening a theatre in the Forsyth Street building, without a
proper license, according to the provisions of an "Act of the Legislature of
the State of New York," and "An Act to Amend An Act to Create a Fund in
Aid of the Society for the Reformation of Juvenile Delinquents in the City
of New York' passed February first in the year one thousand eight hundred
and thirty nine . . . "

The implication is that the Society was the beneficiary of a special bill,
which may have gone largely unenforced, except when it was convenient
to do so. Then, in the Civil War era, at the demand of prominent theatrical managers, the Concert Bill was enacted. The powers granted to the
Society earlier were evidently recalled and turned against concert saloons.
The money was not an issue. The theatre managers were supporting a
worthy charity. And besides, it was a small enough matter to those in control
of the leading playhouses that they would not receive money from the fines,
as long as what they thought of as unfair competion was eliminated.

The recipient of all the fines, then, was the Society for the Reformation
of Juvenile Delinquents. The story of its involvement with the Concert Bill
and a later law goes something like this: all funds collected from fines went
to the highly respectable – and very powerful – Society, not to the city or the
theatres. The reasons seem clear enough. The Society was an organization
whose board contained some of the most prominent names in New York,
people whose rectitude – and often financial power – could not easily be
challenged. And the Society was glad to lend its prestige; compliance was

potentially profitable. But all was not financially well with the Society after the Civil War. It fought back.

In 1872, when the fad for waiter girls was passing, another bill made clear that not only concert saloons but theatres and "other places of performance" still required a license from the Mayor – granted at his discretion. Of considerable significance was one part of the 1872 law, which provided that recipients were required to pay $500 for the license – a large sum of money at the time which, once again, went to the Society. Waiter girls were no longer an issue and were not mentioned.

What constituted a "place of performance" was left unclear, a fact that would be of considerable significance to the money-making potential of the Society for the Reformation of Juvenile Delinquents who once again were the beneficiaries. The established theatres generally paid the license fee more or less automatically, or, at any rate, were left alone. But it was now open season on smaller theatres, the remaining concert saloons, and other places that could not muster powerful allies or the rather exorbitant fee. Many of these small institutions appear in various Society documents, and the Society made a great deal of money from what were apparently quite dubious fines. In 1880, for example, it would make some $35,000 from its licenses and penalties, none of which was publicly accountable.

On the eve of the 1872 law, the police staged a "show" raid on three concert saloons. The Assembly, the Oriental, and the Canterbury had been chosen. The raid was widely discussed in the newspapers of the day. A typical article appeared in an unknown paper on January 23, 1872. Some sixty-five waiter girls and half a dozen other employees, it said, were arrested at a concert saloon (chiefly managers, bartenders, and the like; the police did not arrest any performers). The females were later released, though a point was made that they were generally unrepentant. ("The doors were thrown open and the sixty-five women scampered down Spring Street shouting and laughing, their two hours' incarceration having seemingly had no effect on them.")

But the 1872 law was not accepted unreservedly by the courts. The following news item from the New York *Times* that appeared on February 2, 1872, tells part of the story:

> The proprietors of the three concert-saloons in Broadway, which were recently visited by the Police, were brought up at Special Sessions yesterday, before Justice DOWLING, charged with keeping disorderly houses. The police described the character of these dens and the costume worn by the women, but Justice DOWLING said he could not take the nature

of the costume into consideration at all. The question to decide was, were the houses disorderly, and no acts of a disorderly character having been proved he dismissed the complaints, but directed Capt. MOUNT to make complaint to the Board of Excise, with a view to having the licenses revoked, on the grounds of having sold liquor to minors.

But this did not stop the Society for the Prevention of Juvenile Delinquents. It continued to send in informers. It is the 1872 law that is mentioned most often in the surviving reports of the Society. This was not quite enough; in 1875 and 1876, as we shall see, there were other changes, designed to exclude from protection amateur presentations for charity.

The Society and other reformers, of course, were not objective. Nor was the *Clipper*. They scarcely saw the same places. From the first, in fact, the reformers and the *Clipper* pictured quite different establishments; there was already a kind of *Roshomon*-like quality to descriptions of concert saloons at the time of the Concert Bill and later. The concert saloons, of course, were what they were, but the picture one gave depended in large part on what side of the Concert Bill and later the 1872 bill one was on; that is, whether one agreed with the Society or in fact opposed it and probably violated the various bills. During and after the war, the *Clipper*, for example, seemingly visited no dismal honky-tonks. ("The Boulevard is a very neat and capacious saloon, fitted up with all the paraphernalia of a first-class concert hall"; Lee and Hatstatt's Eureka was a "nice, clean room, painted, papered and oil clothed"). Reformers and the Society visited nothing else but foul dens of iniquity. Depending on their readership, the newspapers essentially were allied with the righteous and were scornful of concert saloons. But on the whole they tended to be somewhat more clear-eyed and realistic than the out-and-out reformers. (The *Police Gazette*, of course, characteristically threw up its hands in horror at what went on in concert saloons, but nudged and winked at the same time.)

An example is the conflicting descriptions of the concert saloon called the Bon Ton, on Broadway between Houston and Bleecker. The account in the *Clipper* emphasized its wholesomeness but James Mc Cabe – an interested party who was superficially a reformer, or at least masqueraded as one – made the place appear to be a low dive. The irony lies in the fact that their descriptions are not very different.

The Bon Ton, said the *Clipper* in 1864, was in a cellar, but was a "well lighted and nicely oil-clothed room," and had "the appearance of an ordinary Broadway drinking saloon." The piece goes on to point out that there was a back room of sorts (probably where the stage was located, though it is not mentioned). "An extensive screen is attached to the end of the bar, about six feet in height and about eighteen in width, painted white. Upon opening the door in same, there was another room, half again as big as the bar, full of females and sightseers paired off at the various veneered tables... On the walls of the Bon Ton are steel portraits of nearly all the celebrated actors, interspersed with some little gems of rural scenery for the lover of nature to contemplate. To those fond of the ridiculous, there are some very good caricatures of crinoline, published in Germany, which are enjoyed just as well by those who wear sixteen steel hoops as the breached lords of creation. They are worth looking at as a momento of the days when women wore crinoline."[8] The reporter adds, "there are no 'private supper rooms,' but all is conducted openly."

In 1868 Mc Cabe saw what was undoubtedly the same place through rather different eyes in *Secrets of the Great City*. (Though, in fairness, the establishment was probably then under different management.) "On Broadway, near — street," he says, "we notice, just above the entrance to the cellar, a flaming transparency, with the inscription 'Madame X—'s Arcade.'" Going down a few steps, Mc Cabe found a large sceen, painted white, with a dancing Venus painted on it. It was the only entrance to the main hall. He and his companion were required to go around it. "We find the floor handsomely covered with matting and oil cloth. On the right hand side, nearest the door is the bar [which is] well furnished, and any drink called for, from beer to champagne, can be instantly obtained."

"A significant feature," Mc Cabe continues provocatively, "is a formidable Colt's revolver, a foot in length, suspended immediately over the sideboard." It was clearly placed there as a warning to the disorderly element. "On the walls are black engravings of the French school [*sic*], fit ornaments for the place... In the back of the hall on a raised platform, is an asthmatic pianoforte, upon which an individual with a threadbare coat, colorless vest, and faded nankeen pantaloons, is thrumming away for dear life."[9] The concert saloon, Mc Cabe says, was filled with loose women and disreputable waiter girls, and was a well-known front for prostitution and assignations.

But a different, more acceptable kind of concert saloon than the Bon Ton was developing in New York after the war. It was aimed at a family audience, and the sources were the German beer garden, as well as traditional male-oriented resorts. Of course, the traditional concert saloon also continued to exist. But after the war, the emphasis of the Society now seemed focused on fines leveled at those institutions that had no proper license from the mayor, regardless of whether they really served alcohol or employed waiter girls. Increasingly, nobody seemed to care much about liquor and waiter girls one way or the other – except, of course, the Society and other social conservatives. The old line that was regularly written into a majority of earlier Society reports – "said audience contained females who sat at tables drinking & conversing with men" – was disappearing. And new accusations were surfacing.

Some concert saloons were always fronts for prostitution. But all in all, many classic New York concert saloons of the Civil War era seem to have offered little more than a relatively brief, pleasant interlude in the drinking. Their story suggests – if it was not clear before – that alcohol – and of course prostitution, where it existed – rather than entertainment was really their first order of business. It continued to be. A free or low-cost show – and waiter girls, when they were a fad – were evidently just inducements to customers to drink their fill in congenial circumstances.

Like the medicine show, the acts may not have been very good. But the show was often offered for the price of a drink served by a pretty waitress, free, or for only a few pennies more. Probably, in some cases, it also acted as prelude to a paid tryst with a prostitute. But not necessarily. Much of the time, it was just drinks that were being sold – and the show and the women who served drinks and undoubtedly sometimes performed seem simply inducements to drink. In any case, the fact is that, like the medicine show, the concert-saloon show represented one of the beginnings of the use of entertainment as an advertising device.

2

Changes in direction: the concert saloon
after the war

That the interior of said building was fitted up in a manner ... as are usual in theatres, concert rooms, "gardens" and places where theatrical, minstrel, and other public performances of the character above specified are exhibited.

Blank form, 1873, filled out for Variens Halle, 208 East Houston Street

FOLLOWING THE END OF THE CIVIL WAR, ENTERTAINMENT in New York was changing in important ways. The military had largely disappeared from the city. And public attitudes were changing for good, too; the city was becoming increasingly liberal and realistic in its point of view. As a result, for many men, the old fashioned male-oriented concert saloon – along with waiter girls – was ceasing to be a fad, and much of the need for a prestigious organization to oppose it was beginning to come to an end.

The decline of the male-oriented concert saloons had also probably been hastened, among other things, by the "modernization" of an existing entertainment form, the German beer garden. As the century progressed, German beer gardens, both indoor and outdoor, had begun to widen their scope, trying to attract native English-speaking family audiences. William Schwab, the owner of the Harlem Bridge Concert Garden, at 2387 Third Avenue, claimed in 1884 that his establishment was intended as "a respectable and enjoyable resort for those of my countrymen, *and others* [italics mine], that desired to visit it with their families." The famous old Atlantic Garden, perhaps the best known German beer garden, began to advertise itself in more contemporary terms in 1882 as "The Only Genuine Family Resort in America." The concert-saloon owners were watching with interest.

Increasingly, concert saloons offering shows were becoming more like the beer gardens. Family orientation made business sense. Trial balloons had probably already appeared as early as the sixties, when matinees for ladies first took place in some concert saloons. By the late seventies and early eighties, a number now welcomed "respectable" women, and indeed whole families. Zellers, in his 1968 article, talks about some of the early changes:

> Several of the more prominent concert saloons...hoping to put their idle daytime hours to profit, offered matinees aimed at the family trade. The earliest record that I have found of such a matinee appears in the *Clipper* for May 5, 1860: an ad for Frank Rivers' Melodeon in Philadelphia announces a "G R A N D   M A T I N E E . . . S A T U R D A Y   A F T E R N O O N, M A Y 5th for the accommodation of F A M I L I E S   A N D   C H I L D R E N." Similar afternoon performances were offered at about the same time at such popular New York resorts as the Canterbury, the Broadway Music Hall, and the American Concert Hall.

Zellers goes on to point out that:

> Most resorts advertised that all drinking and smoking would be forbidden during the matinee. The Broadway Music Hall, for example, announced in Wilkes' *Spirit of the Times* on June 8, 1861: "A Grand Matinee, every Saturday afternoon at 2 o'clock, for the accommodation of Ladies and Children, on which occasion the bars will be closed, and no liquor or cigars will be sold or permitted to be used in the theatre."[1]

Zellers continues, giving his findings. "The only information that I have uncovered about the nature of the matinee performance itself," he says, "is an undated program for the Canterbury that announces a 'Ladies Matinee every Saturday when all choice Gems of the evening performance will be given.'" (According to posters on its walls, there was a matinee of *some* kind in 1879 at the Newport, at two o'clock on every Monday and Thursday.) Just how successful such matinees were at the time, Zellers claims not to know since "journalistic remarks about the matinees are rare and relatively uninformative." But the fact that the matinee idea was to become a regular feature at many resorts suggests that the afternoon shows were at least drawing satisfactory family business.

Of course, the result was that, after the war, the Society for the Prevention of Juvenile Delinquency was left with a dwindling source of revenue. A symbol of the fact that the Society was losing control of performance activities – and money – was the fact that, for a while, it was forced to share the profits from its fines with the Actors' Fund. The answer to not sharing seemed to lie with the 1872 bill.

In 1872, in fact, the Society's powers had been, if anything, enlarged. The bill could be interpreted to mean that the Society could recommend to the City that all sorts of places – not just concert saloons – could now be closed down if they did not have proper licenses to present performances. And – conveniently – what was and was not a performance was defined – however vaguely – by the Society for the Prevention of Juvenile Delinquency.

As a result of the somewhat amorphous powers given to the Society by the legislators, it now became more interested in other kinds of entertainment establishments. The Society sent investigators into family-oriented concert saloons; beer gardens; medicine shows; small theatres; variety houses; rental halls of various kinds, often the sites of illegal benefits or other shows; the so-called lecture rooms of dime museums; and other places of amusement, which, it said, had no proper license for performance.

The proposed fines and closings of these establishments often do indeed seem far-fetched, a "desperate exercise of failing power" on the part of the Society. As Charles Byrne, the editor of the *Dramatic News*, pointed out on December 25, 1880, if anyone connected with the Society for the Reformation of Juvenile Delinquents, walking down the street, heard a piano playing in any public building, the organization would immediately serve a summons on the proprietor for not having a proper license to present a show.

Indeed, there is little reason to think that many of the places the Society investigated in the eighties and nineties promoted juvenile delinquency – or prostitution or excessive alcohol consumption, for that matter. But the Society for the Prevention of Juvenile Delinquents sent in investigators anyway, in some cases referring in their documents to the places as concert saloons when obviously they were not. In any case, the more stringent the enforcement and the more frequent the prosecutions under it, the more money the Society continued to take in, and the more it could claim publicly that it was fulfilling its mission, however cloudy it was.

The function of the institutions that the Society investigated is not always clear today from the records that remain, although it is obvious that the majority were certainly not traditional male-oriented concert saloons – even though they were sometimes referred to in that way in Society documents. Still, these institutions were now easy targets of the Society; they did not have an expensive theatrical license from the City. And that was grist for the Society's mill. By stretching matters a little, it could be concluded that any number of establishments were in violation of the 1872 law on some grounds or other. (Waiter girls, of course, were fast becoming ancient history in New York. But something could be found.)

The smaller, less powerful institutions, especially, were ripe for the Society's attentions, whether or not they actually contributed to low morals among the citizens or to juvenile delinquency in the City. They lacked political and financial power. Almost certainly, however, most did not corrupt the morals of patrons – at least, not in any very significant way. The ploy more or less worked, however; when a new City administration came to power, the Society continued to benefit from fines. It received them until its disappearance in the early twentieth century.

A number of institutions protested that they should not be subject to the Society's attentions. As early as 1878, a proprietor made clear that he was doing nothing wrong and that the Society for the Reformation of Juvenile Delinquents had no right to fine him and recommend that his establishment be closed. They had never seen any performances on the premises. A witness confirmed his story and pointed out that he too had never seen any performances on the premises except "singing [by customers] and piano playing. That no admission fee is charged [and that there is] no sign or other advertisement or notice, indicating that any performance was carried on or conducted at said premises." In fact, he had not seen anything going on that was different from "any other Bier Saloon in this City." Most of the summonsed, however, seemed not to bother with very strong protests knowing that they had little chance of proving their case.

Of course, some variations of the old-fashioned, male-oriented concert saloons continued to exist and continued to undergo the scrutiny of the Society, as in the past. A good example was a place called The Bowery Varieties, 33 Bowery, which the Society attempted to have fined and closed in 1879 and again in 1882. A Society report specified that the interior of the building included a raised stage, footlights, a drop curtain, both a flat (probably a backdrop of some kind) and side scenes, as well as a musical group consisting of piano, violin, cornet, and drums. One document from 1879 seemingly hedged its bets by calling The Bowery Varieties a "concert room and theatre." Probably, the building simply housed a somewhat old-fashioned concert saloon; though perhaps there was also a kind of variety theatre with abundant alcohol on the site, or a house of prostitution.

In any event, in that year, The Bowery Varieties presented a show featuring four men and four women, appearing in minstrel-show fashion. The four were in costume, the women in plush dresses, tights, and fancy shoes, the men acting as "endmen," playing respectively the tambourine and bones and dressed in costume and wearing blackface. The group sang two songs and told jokes, recited puns, and gave various recitations. This act was followed by a "musical interlude," by what the report called "the orchestra," and a song and dance by two blacked-up males (perhaps two of the men who had appeared in the first act). Then came another act that featured songs, dances, and acrobatics by three males, one of whom appeared in drag. Maybe it was also presented by some of the same men. In any case, the acts were advertised by posters in the street in front of the Bowery Varieties, and about one-hundred-fifty people were in the audience. On another evening, the investigator reported, the show featured a female singer in a short dress, colored stockings, and fancy shoes, who waltzed up and down the stage. That show also contained a clog dance by a male in blackface. About a hundred people were in attendance.

Although in 1882 the Society reports were calling the place a theatre, it is impossible to know whether the building had actually become more or less a variety theatre or whether the Society had simply found it convenient to muddy the distinction further. Probably it was basically still a traditional male-oriented concert saloon since a note in the May 2, 1882 Society citation pointed out that admission was free, that "some females [sat] at tables drinking and smoking with men." "Private Boxes" – possibly a code for prostitution on the premises – were mentioned in one report.

The show on May 2, 1882 included an unnamed song by a female, who also sang "The Pitcher of Beer," encoring it with the last part of the unnamed song. This was followed by another tune, "Awfully Awful," sung by another woman, "attired in fancy costume," who danced at the end of each verse. Then came music by the "orchestra" and another unnamed song. The show ended with another woman singing "A Violet from My Mother's Grave."

A second place, the Sultan Divan, 241 Bowery, was probably another traditional male-oriented concert saloon. The Sultan Divan was investigated by the Society in 1881 and again in the following year. (The term "waiter girl" seems no longer to have been used; one of the documents refers to "waitresses." Advertising flyers referred to them as "beautiful bar maids"). In any event, The Sultan Divan seems to have contained a stage, and several documents speak darkly of "private boxes," and "many females, some of whom sat at tables drinking and conversing with male companions." Other females appeared on stage, in a fairly routine free show, which from time to time during these years also included minstrel sketches, performed by male actors who had their hands and faces blackened.

But family-oriented German beer gardens were among those that were also attacked, sometimes as traditional concert saloons (which they were not). For example, Ferdinand Goebel's Casino, 163 and 165 East Fifty-ninth

Street, probably a relatively innocuous family-oriented resort, still catering to Germans, was cited several times in 1884 for a show that followed the main lines of the following:

> Song in the German language by a female who was dressed in costume – piano accompaniment played by a male performer. Being recalled she sang another song in German language accompanied as before.

> Musical selections played on the piano by a male performer.

> Comic song in the German language by another female who was attired in gaudy costume. Piano accompaniment.

> Musical selections played on the piano by a male performer.

> Song in German language by another female – piano accompaniment.

> Being encored she sang another German song. Piano accompaniment.

> Musical selections played on the piano by a male performer.[2]

Many of the places brought into court by the Society were, as in the past, ultra respectable, and typically offering a kind of "pops concert," often of well-known musical classics, rather than "low" music and other variety acts. Among the features that the brewer and saloon owner Jacob Ruppert presented in 1882 at his place on the north-east corner of Third Avenue and Ninety-first Street, for example, was "an orchestra composed of five females and two males, four of said females playing violins, the other playing the violincello; one of the males played the violone [a variation of the violin] and the other played the piano. Said orchestra is advertised as the 'World-Famed Karlsbader Ladies Orchestra.'" At intervals a singer offered German songs and the "Ladies Orchestra" presented selections from *Martha* and *The Bohemian Girl,* and, for an encore, a medley of "Way Down Upon the Swanee River," "The Star-Spangled Banner," "Hail, Columbia," and "Yankee Doodle."

But the German establishments were not the only targets of the Society. As time went on, amateur performances (often for the benefit of the organization itself) also grew far more attractive. As the Society looked around for unlicensed performances, some of these amateurs offered an easy target. In 1875 and again in 1876, for example, it made certain that amateur performances, not for specifically religious purposes, were not exempted from its scrutiny. An 1876 claim was made by the Society against the Masonic lodge, a bold stroke, indeed. In the early eighties it asserted its rather ambiguous claims once more, saying that a certain performance was fair game because it was "not given by amateurs for the benefit of any church, mission, parish, or Sunday school or for any other charitable purpose . . . "

The sites of many of these unauthorized performances were the halls rented out to amateur groups in the city. There were many of these halls, among them some rather grand places, more or less fully equipped theatres, like Steinway Hall, near Union Square, that were rented both to professionals and the more prosperous non-profit groups. The Society investigated a few such prominent groups and places, but most probably they had too many powerful supporters to be truly vulnerable.

More typical perhaps were the modest flat-floor halls, often with a simple stage at one end, used for amateur theatricals by the less affluent organizations. These groups – and the halls that housed them – were the ones that the Society most often observed and fined, and that the City most often closed down. In 1880, for example, it took a baleful interest in a production of an original pageant called *Under the Yoke, Or Bond and Free!*, and in a sketch by the same author, "Fun in An Elevated Station," advertised and presented at Manhattan Hall by "The Colored Employees of the Manhattan Elevated Railway." Two years earlier, Baker's Central Hall claimed that the performances there should be exempt from the restrictions on amateurs imposed by the Society and that, in any case, the hall was primarily "a ball room and meeting room."

The halls, of course, were also used by professional showmen. An especially interesting example was John E. Healy and Charlie Bigelow's entertainment, which took place in Harlem Hall, at 125 East One-hundred-twenty-fifth Street. It may well have been an early version of the famous medicine shows later sent on the road from New Haven by Healy and Bigelow. At least, it is known that in later years the pair ultimately became rich and famous by combining the American public's interest in Indians and free variety shows, with the sale of patent medicines between the acts.

Although medicine sales are not mentioned by the Society, the free show presented in New York City sounds remarkably like the duo's later efforts at sponsored medicine-show entertainment. The hall, according to the Society, had a stage in it on which scenery belonging either to Healy and Bigelow or the owner – or a mixture of both – was set up. On the floor next to the stage was an organ. Three hundred people were in attendance. Although it was labeled a concert hall in Society documents, there is no indication that any alcohol (other than what was contained in the Kickapoo Indian Sagwa and other remedies) was sold to patrons. The show

the Society investigated on December 29, 1883, resembled the combination
of Indian and variety material that Healy and Bigelow later were to make
famous:

> Songs by a number of Indians who were dressed in costume.
>
> Tumbling and acrobatic performances, by two male performers who were
> dressed in costume.
>
> Dancing by six Indians who were dressed in costume. Performance of
> jugglry and prestidigitation by a male performer. Said performance in-
> cluded tricks with cards, hats, and ropes.
>
> Acrobatic performances on the horizontal bar by two male performers
> who were dressed in fancy costumes, and acting the part of a clown. In
> response to an encore the said performers repeated the last above described
> performances, organ accompaniment.
>
> Snake dance by six Indians in costume.
>
> A dramatic sketch or farce representing a scene in a boarding house,
> performed by three males who were dressed in costume adapted to the
> character of the piece and who represented parts or characters therein.[3]

There are many more examples of the use of halls by professional showmen. As early as 1873, for example, a magic show (probably presented by a
professional) at the highly respectable Steinway Hall, drew the attention of
the Society because no license had been obtained. Indeed, the investigation
of halls was routine after the middle seventies, in the face of the fact that
halls continued to insist that they did not present shows as such – only entertainment for their members and guests, or *bona fide* concerts – and thus
were not liable to fines and closure.

In 1879, for instance, Tyrolian Halle, obviously an institution catering
to a German clientele, presented an event clearly billed as a concert in the
New Yorker Staats Zeitung of October 19. "The most beautiful family resort
in the city," it read, would be presenting, "Every night during the week,"
a "Grand Vocal and Instrumental Concert." It was to be "Given by the
Celebrated Tyrolian Alpine Singers" and featured "Ladies and 3 Gentlemen
in National Costume," as well as S. Geschwandrer, an expert on the zither
and something called the "violin-zither." But it all did no good. As far as the
Society was concerned, the hall was yet another place where "minstrelsy and
other public performances" took place, and thus was liable for not having a
theatrical license.

The dime museum, as noted in the Prologue, was an important tourist institution. Like the halls, it catered to families and was generally considered harmless, except by the most conservative. Many of these proprietary museums contained so-called lecture rooms, in which curiosities, variety performers, and the occasional highly moral play appeared. Usually professional actors or other professional performers worked there. But no alcohol was available and the offerings were considered suitable for ladies and children. In large part, the lecture rooms at dime museums, like the museums themselves, were aimed at rather genteel and unsophisticated family audiences, people who were not very likely to attend theatres as such, but found it perfectly acceptable to see a show in a popular "educational" context – in spite of the fact that it contained somewhat dubious theatre people. Unknown to them, there probably was some exchange of performers, routines, and sketches between classic male-oriented concert saloons and dime museums, although the museums characteristically rewrote and presented only "clean" material. By the early eighties, the Society was taking on these lecture rooms, as well as amateur performances in halls. In 1881, for example, the Society tried to close the London Museum, ostensibly because its lecture room featured a magic show, a puppet show, and – a precursor of the movies – a magic lantern show.

Waiter girls were old hat, and presumably not much of an issue in New York by the early eighties. And, of course, alcohol was available in most theatres of all kinds, and the theatres were now answerable to the Society. Many small playhouses actually served alcohol in the auditorium during performances, or were located next to a saloon, sometimes with a connecting door. A chapter in a book published in 1886, *Theatrical and Circus Life*, by John J. Jennings says that "the wine room, which is an adjunct of all these houses . . . is a place that affords seclusion to those that want to be out of the way of meeting friends or attracting the notice of strangers."[4]

Though alcohol and waiter girls were no longer of paramount importance to the Society in the decades after the war, "legitimate" theatres, and opera houses with professional performers were vulnerable if they had no proper license for a show – the alliance between the Society and theatre people seems to have been long forgotten. A few of those chosen for scrutiny were prominent venues like the famous Booth's Theatre on Fourteenth Street or Wallack's. These, however, were questionable targets, since, as in the case of the large halls, their owners and managers often had money to spend on lawyers and important political connections. It appears, though, that the big theatres receiving the Society's scrutiny housed unlicensed attractions of some importance. The Society was enlisted to help drive attractions out, very likely at the behest of prominent New Yorkers. An example was *The Passion,* a controversial play about the passion of Christ, written by the eccentric Salmi Morse. *The Passion* had already caused controversy during its production in San Francisco, and a number of people in New York (including some ministers and members of the city council) were worried about its potential appearance in their city in 1883. A number of them were determined that *The Passion* would never open in New York.

The building was a former church that later had been used as a livery stable and a national guard armory. Morse altered it for theatrical production in about November of 1882, adding such features as a gallery, a large stage on the north side of the building, and an organ on its west side. The auditorium and gallery seated some 1,500 people. Morse said that his building was not a theatre but a hall, even claiming on one occasion that it was a church.

It all made little difference, however; the Society apparently was successful in helping to drive out the play. Among other things, an investigator from the Society entered the building during its alteration, looked around, and talked to Morse, who allowed him to attend a rehearsal. He said in his report that *The Passion* "is as much a stage drama as any ordinarily produced at theatres in the City of New York and is tragedy in all essential features of said class of drama." In any event, the group apparently did its best. *The Passion did* open, but only for one performance. It held a free, invited dress rehearsal at Morse's theatre on Twenty-third Street on March 30, 1883.

Most of the theatres slated for scrutiny by the Society were cheap houses, however, on or around the Bowery, or in other inexpensive entertainment districts. Largely they presented melodramas or popular operas. The Society documents are silent as to why it picked the places it did; probably they were chosen because they were *not* particularly powerful and presumably would not put up too strenuous a legal battle. One of them seems to have been the Bijou Opera House, which, in 1880, presented a "comic opera in three acts," called *The Mascotte* by a minor composer named Audran, with the "Lambert Children" introducing "their original violin specialties" in the second act.

In 1884, the Cosmopolitan Theatre, 1445 Broadway, was brought into court for presenting another of Audran's works, *Olivette.* Another house was the Third Avenue Theatre, which, apparently without a license, presented "a large group of actors and actresses" in a comedy called *Our Bachelors,* with "all the usual costumes and characterizations." A third was the Mount Morris Theatre which, in 1883, was accused of unauthorized productions of *M'Liss,* using as partial proof the fact that the theatre advertised the performances in the *New York Herald* of May 23.

Another of the forms often investigated by the Society in the eighties was the small-time variety theatre. Variety theatres served alcohol but of course they were *not* traditional concert saloons and should not be confused with them. Many of them were "fast," and a number contained bars, of course – some even allowed alcohol to be taken into the auditoriums. Unlike concert saloons, however, the bars in these variety theatres were not the primary reason for the institutions' existence. They were simply activities *in support* of entertainment, rather than a primary reason for the place.

Variety, however, was on the rise at the time, and cheap variety theatres, catering to both men and women were common on the Bowery and in other entertainment districts throughout the city. Variety came in a number of different guises and is hard to define. It is clear, however, that, like the concert saloon, they influenced both vaudeville and burlesque. Basically, the variety houses that flourished from the Civil War era to perhaps the 1890s, differed from one another but seem to have specialized in individual acts offered by various members of a stock company; they presented acts rather than being organized around full-length plays, as were most of the so-called "legitimate" theatres.

Dora Barrett, the old San Francisco actress who appeared in popular forms in the West, makes clear in her memoirs a useful distinction between variety and vaudeville. "Variety," she says, "was the forerunner of vaudeville . . . From my vantage point, I offer, based on my personal observations, the following explanation":

> In variety the same people remained at the theater, as a stock company. Each week, they sang different songs, wore different costumes, presented different dances, and, in general varied their acts. By contrast, in vaudeville, different performers came to a theatre for a week or two's engagement. The formats in both were similar. The vaudevillians were singers, dancers, acrobats, et al [*sic*], doing the specialties for that week. At the conclusion of their engagement they moved on to yet another theater or town; and a new group would replace them, doing pretty much the same thing, but with new people doing it.[5]

A bill from a fairly typical small New York variety house, the Athenaeum 585, on Broadway, opposite the Metropolitan Hotel – undated but undoubtedly from the 1870s – makes the point. The Athenaeum featured a serio-comic singer, comedians (both male and female), blackface, Irish, and Dutch

4 Bill from a New York variety theatre, September 16, 1873 comedy, a sketch entitled "Going to the Races," another called "The Actor's Studio," others called "Troubles in a Pawn Shop" and "Louisa's Courtship," supposed "Mid-Air Flights," dancer-singers, banjoists, the principal burlesque, called "Ernani, or the Horns of a Dilemma! In six scenes and a powerful chorus," as well as the Worrell Sisters, and the "re-appearance of the Comet of 1873, Miss Leona Dare . . . Matinees Wednesday and Saturday afternoons at two o'clock, admission 25 cents to five dollars for a box, children admitted to the matinee at half price." The fare in many variety houses like this one was probably not very different from that in many small concert saloons.

The Society evidently employed with variety houses the same principle that it used with theatres and other institutions: it was most effective to attack small ones that were not well known and could probably not afford effective legal representation. In 1881 the Society investigated the Bowery Garden Theatre, a small playhouse at 113 and 113 1/2 Bowery, charging twenty-five cents admission and offering a variety bill featuring a contortionist, minstrel sketches, a quick-change artist, various singers, and, at times, a truncated – and almost certainly pirated – version of the scandalous play *Mazeppa*, in which Adah Isaacs Menken had appeared, apparently naked, in 1861, or a Western melodrama called *Abe, the Pioneer, or the Mad Hunter of Arizona*.

The Alhambra Theatre, 124–125 West Twenty-seventh Street, was also investigated. It featured unremarkable attractions, including:

> Overture played by the orchestra. Sentimental Ballad sung by a female attired in fancy costume, chorus by the other members of the company – orchestral accompaniment.

> Comic song sung by a male performer, who was blackened to represent a negro, and dressed in grotesque costume – while singing he accompanied himself on the 'bones' – orchestral accompaniment also sentimental song by another minstrel named Wood – orchestral accompaniment, chorus in which the other members joined – comic song by another minstrel who accompanied himself on the tambourine, orchestral accompaniment also – said minstrel was blackened to represent a negro and was dressed in grotesque costume.

> Song by a female who was dressed in fancy costume, orchestral accompaniment. Duet by a male and female.[6]

In the decades after the war, then, there seems to have been a concerted movement toward the polite show. The shows presented in beer gardens, restaurants, small theatres, and other venues, appear not to have been very different from those presented in many concert saloons and pioneered by Tony Pastor at his Fourteenth Street Theatre, opened in 1881, whose later presentations are often seen as the precursor of "clean" vaudeville. Pastor, a former circus performer, had been owner or manager of several unsuccessful variety theatres aimed at family audiences. He finally succeeded with the Fourteenth Street Theatre.

Like Pastor, managers and owners of concert saloons were probably less concerned with moral reform than with the possibilities that lay in attracting an audience that was more than double the size of the traditional male-oriented one. The Society papers suggest, at any rate, that new up-market places that moved in the direction of German beer gardens with a difference – family-oriented, English-language entertainment that could not offend even the most fastidious; and these scrupulously clean acts had begun to appear in earnest by the late seventies and early eighties. Probably they were already common currency in many concert saloons. The fact that these new places appeared and were generally accepted had created serious problems for the Society.

The Society, in fact, seems to have become something of a victim of its own dubious success. All in all, between the end of the Civil War and about the mid-eighties, it evidently did not confine itself to sending its inspectors into troublesome concert saloons – only by a stretch of the imagination its mission anyway. But it moved in new directions. The pickings were growing slimmer with the end of the war, the departure of many troops from New York City, the dimunition of the waiter-girl craze – and with changing attitudes in the City.

The evidence is confusing and difficult to interpret. But, especially after 1872, it appears that, in order to keep a source of revenue, the Society chose to investigate a number of different kinds of establishment that had liquor licenses but no theatrical licenses, and which offered patrons some form of entertainment. Often, in addition to classic concert saloons, these were innocuous German beer gardens, or small "legitimate," musical or variety theatres that, in spirit at least, may have been, if not especially elevating, acceptable to most people in New York, as concert saloons were probably not.

3

Concert-saloon acts

Beer, boys, beer, is the liquor we should stick to,
  Beer, boys, beer, of a well reputed brand;
Beer, boys, beer, no more of idle sorrow,
  At six cents a pint now it sparkles through the land.

From a concert-saloon song

BETWEEN THE MID-SIXTIES AND THE MID-EIGHTIES FEW important changes took place in the kinds of acts presented in New York concert saloons. But there were some. By and large, many owners and managers seem to have been cautious during the war and for a while after, confining themselves largely to musical routines – often performed by customers – which they thought were more or less legal. But they found that even musical acts were in dispute as far as the Society and the City were concerned. And that the fad for waiter girls was declining. As a result, many traditional places gradually drifted away and became family-oriented. But some stuck with male-oriented concert saloons, though waiter girls were no longer so much in evidence.

Increasingly, both types seemed to include variety turns that were not musical, and mostly fairly innocuous. What is clear is that many owners and managers of concert saloons were consciously violating the rather ambiguous spirit of the various bills. But perhaps they were willing to do so because of the extra fees sometimes charged for entertainment, from the increased alcohol sold, or, in some cases, from a sideline of prostitution. Or because they misinterpreted the rather convoluted meaning of the bills. Or possibly because they had some "arrangement" with the City or the investigators from the Society which kept them from being raided or fined. At any rate, it brought in patrons.

Initially, however, cautious proprietors often confined their entertainments to songs or some other species of innocuous musical activity. The Novelty Concert Hall, 616 Broadway, for example, which was probably underneath another well-known concert saloon, the Gaieties, announced somewhat obsequiously in the *Herald* in April of 1862 that, "We bow in humble submission to our wise legislators in Albany, and substitute for our late concert room performances a grand Industrial Musical Entertainment by two full bands – Jackson's Brass Band and Blythe's String Band. Admission Free."

But technically, even this act was probably a violation of the Concert Bill, if waiter girls were present – as they may have been at the Novelty. Owners and managers who were particularly anxious about fines and imprisonment made sure that no waiter girls were in evidence, and organized purely amateur events, "sing songs" or so-called "harmonic evenings," where patrons were induced to sing for one another. "Sing songs" of various kinds had existed long before the Concert Bill and, they reasoned, could scarcely be thought of as performances.

According to the *Herald* of March 11, 1862, there was a "grand Harmonic meeting" at a concert saloon at 107 Grand Street every evening, featuring one Walter Smith at the piano, as well as a bar "stocked with the best of Ales, Wines, Liquors, and Segars." For a while, there were countless variations. After the Concert Bill, some saloons, like the Bon Ton and Ballard's What Is It, at 600 Broadway, between Prince and Houston, still had only a piano that seemingly was played by customers.

At the Bon Ton in 1864 there apparently was only a piano for entertainment, and customers who sang. "The man from Lake Lomand," noted the *Clipper*, "after warbling the air of a tune to himself, volunteered to sing the praises of his 'Bonnie Annie, blithe and gay'; and as he warmed to his work, by his pantomimic motions it is evident that he imagined himself once more in the land of the shamrocks [*sic*] ganging aw' o'er the heath to the village with his lassie as a companion."[1]

In the mid-sixties, at the St. Nicholas Casino, underneath the St. Nicholas Hotel at 509 Broadway, the *Clipper* noted that both a piano and several violins were present, probably played by professionals, although the singers were amateurs. First came an Irish customer. Initially, said the *Clipper*, "Mr. Red Shirt declined; but when the light haired, beardless pianist struck up 'The Wild Irish Boy,' and the bewhiskered Teutons commenced making their cat gut talk in the same strain, Belden [presumably the Irishman] couldn't refrain. And he sang it right through better than one is accustomed to hear at sing-songs and harmonic meetings. Of course he got the encore. He then gave a musical recitation from the French, composed by De Briantio and sung at his opera house nightly. It is all about the Little Old Market Woman and her dog . . . "[2] An old market woman fell asleep on the highway and had her petticoat cut off while she slept. The song ended as follows:

> Home went the little woman all in the dark,
> Out came the little dog and he began to bark,
> The dog began to bark and she began to cry,
> 'Lord a 'massy on me, I know 'taint I.

In 1864, the Occidental may well have had both music *and* waiter girls, who spent at least part of their time performing. The veteran Wiliam Allen had both a piano and violin at the Occidental. "Taking a look around the internal arrangements," wrote the *Clipper*, "we noticed a piano fixed plumb up against the windows facing the street – rather a cold place in the winter time – with a very nice looking girl seated thereat; and by her side sat a violinist. While the latter fiddled the former played upon the grand pianner."[3] The *Clipper* also noted that Frank Burns' Oriental, 650 Broadway, between Bleecker and Bond, featured a piano and violin.

Sometimes, waiter girls who "happened to be present" were encouraged to volunteer to sing, in the somewhat vain hope that they qualified as "amateur" performers. There were many variations. The song by the Irish patron at the St. Nicholas Casino, for example, was followed by a waiter girl, who was brought in to sing what sounds like a minstrel song:

> Sally has got a lubly nose,
> Flat across her face it grows,
> It sounds like thunder when it blows,
> Such a lubly nose has Sally!
>
> She can smell a rat,
> So mind where you're at,
> It's rader sharp although it's flat,
> Is de lubly nose of Sally.
>
>   Sally come up! oh! Sally go down,
> Sally come twist your heels around;
> De old man he's gone down to town,
> Oh! Sally come down the middle![4]

5 Lithograph sheet music covers of two sentimental songs performed in concert saloons in the 1880s and published in the 1870s: "Take This Letter to My Mother" and "I Have No Home"

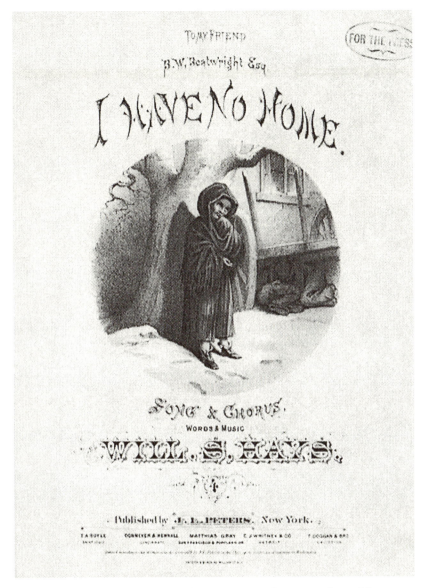

6 Lithograph sheet music covers of two sentimental songs performed in concert saloons in the 1880s and published in the 1870s: "Take This Letter to My Mother" and "I Have No Home"

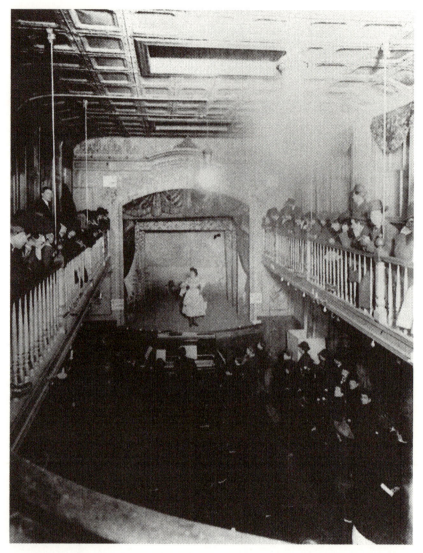

7 Photograph of a New York City concert saloon or variety house, n.d.

Sometimes, said the *Clipper*, the musicians sang. Lee and Hatstatt's Eureka, 544 Broadway, still had only a piano in 1874, "played by one of the Smith family," who seem to have been professional musicians. At length "Mr. Smith [perhaps Walter again] was persuaded into singing a Dutch [German] song which was translated into English as near as our limited language of the Faderland would admit." The song was printed with the *Clipper* article:

Song of a Swiper
Beer boys, beer, is the liquor we should stick to,
    Beer, boys, beer, of a well reputed brand;
Beer, boys, beer, no more of idle sorrow,
    At six cents a pint now it sparkles through the land.

Beer, boys, beer, a jug of honest swizzle,
    Beer, boys, beer, we get it for a groat;
Beer, boys, beer, 'Tis pleasant to reflect that
    At six cents a pint it gurgles in the throat.

Beer, boys, beer, at six cents for a drink, boys,
    Beer, boys, beer, at six cents for a soak;
Beer, boys, beer, how pleasant 'tis to think, boys,
    That four men for a quarter can all enjoy a joke![5]

Some of the shows had more or less professional – and probably illegal – masters-of-ceremonies in the manner of British music halls. The Melodeon, 563 Broadway, near Prince Street, for example, had one who doubled as a pianist and fiddle player, as well as a comic singer. "Young Solomons, son of the old gentleman and an excellent tenor," runs the *Clipper* account, in 1864 "is a good card and extremely useful withal, for if the 'piannerist' or 'fiddlerist' or any other ist happens to get taken down sick, Mose takes his posish and the show goes on. He is a sort of Monsieur Boulcourt – calls out the names of the singers, raps for order and raps for applause. His style is melodramatic, if you know what that means. Or he can take a hand at the comic if necessary, always careful to avoid bawdy-house songs, which is more than we can say of some free-and-easies."[6]

An innocuous imitation of a calliope took place at several concert saloons, including the Garden, 45 Great Jones Street, as late as 1880. Surely that could not be illegal. But it was all to no avail. The Society was powerful enough so that it could always find something wrong with almost anything.

But there were always challenges from the concert saloons. As early as 1864, the large and rather important 444 had called itself "the only management with sufficient energy, courage, independence, and manliness to contest the constitutionality and justice of the Concert Bill." Its owners truculently advertised in the *Herald* that Tony Pastor, Charlie White, and other professional entertainers would appear. In March of 1864, the Metropolitan was consciously violating the Concert Bill, presenting a "wonder" on the tight rope, Mlle. Rosa.

Four-forty-four was not entirely alone. During the last years of the war, it is true, many of the concert saloons still in business featured musical routines, but, as time went on, a number apparently were also to employ more non-musical acts rather openly. By 1872 another bill had been passed in Albany, which informed saloon owners that they could not give a show without an expensive license from the mayor, although nowhere were waiter girls mentioned. It was apparently designed to expand and modernize the earlier bill, in order to keep raising revenue for the Society. In addition to items listed in 1862, it also added that a venue must have a license from the City – vetted by the Society's investigators – to present "any equestrian, circus, or dramatic performance, or any performance of jugglers, or rope-dancing, acrobats." But the Society would tackle almost anything. The idea already had been a successful source of revenue. Now any act which appeared in concert saloons or any other kind of unlicensed theatre was fair game for the Society and the City.

What exactly did the 1872 bill mean? A clear-cut answer was not forth-coming – probably intentionally – from either the Society or the politicians, and various entertainment people – not just people associated with tradi-tional male-oriented concert saloons – were hauled into court. At the same time, of course, there were always out-of-work minstrel, variety, and other popular performers and those who wanted to supplement their salaries by appearing in traditional concert saloons. Thus, some of the material done there – both musical and otherwise – clearly followed that seen in other popular theatres of all kinds.

In fact, entertainers of many different sorts were willing to take the chance that their act could squeak by. Why not? Or they simply did not care. A number of them performed in several different concert saloons, over the years. Many of these had English-sounding names (The Brighton, for example, and the London Music Hall, 455 Sixth Avenue). One concert saloon, the Bowery Music Hall, 20 Bowery, in 1879, is known to have fea-tured what was undoubtedly a knockoff on the popular British Blondes, called "The Lady Show," hedging its bets with a minstrel troupe and five-cent schooners of Lion Beer.

Some traditional concert saloons, like The Academy of Fun, Broome and Broadway, had shows "every evening except Sundays." A flyer from Batch-elor's Music Hall, 27 Bowery, undated, but presumably from the seventies, presented shows "Every Evening at Eight o'clock Precisely." On the other hand, time and again the investigators comment that performances took place, to the best of their knowledge, "at least every Saturday evening," as was the case at O'Donnell's (or Gramercy Hall), at 230 Third Avenue, in 1875.

A number of the routines presented at such places – comic sketches and the like – undoubtedly had their origins in variety, or perhaps in British music hall. Although because of the vague descriptions, we cannot know for sure whether they may first have begun in other forms of popular entertainment. In any case, similarity between variety theatre acts and those presented at concert saloons seems to have been assumed. (Not that they were the only places where time-honored acts could be seen.)

In 1875 at a traditional concert saloon, O'Donnells or Gramercy Hall, the investigators pointed out "that said performances were similar in many respects to those exhibited at 'Variety Theatres' in this City." At Centennial Gardens in 1876, the performance "was similar to those exhibited at the average Variety Theatre," and at Clinton Garden in the following year, the investigator remarked "that said performances were what are termed 'Variety' performances." At Clinton Garden in 1877 there was "minstrelsy and dancing [whether by performers or patrons we do not know], and what were ordinarily known as 'Variety' performances." Batchelor's Music Hall advertised a "Grand Variety Entertainment."

Professional entertainers of any sort had in fact been barred from working in concert saloons as early as the Concert Bill, perhaps earlier. But, like the Bill itself, just what defined a professional entertainer was not very clear; the evidence is mostly based on the *Clipper* series, and it is possible that the agreement to write the articles implied a requirement to conceal some of the illegalities taking place. But in 1872, professionals seem to have been resolutely banned from working in concert saloons and other institutions that had no license from the City.

Time after time, the Society papers included something like this statement in an 1877 report about the American Hall, 15 Bowery: "The said minstrels [as performers were called in the Society's papers] are professional and receive compensation for their services as deponent is informed and believes." Another document from 1877, regarding the investigation of Clinton Garden, stipulates that "said performances were not given by amateurs for the benefit of any church, parish, mission or Sunday school, or for any charitable or religious purpose." A note appeared in the file of McHugh's Free and Easy, at 65 West Houston Street, in the same year. "As deponent is informed and believes," it read, "all of said minstrels are professionals and as such are employed by and receive compensation from said defendant McHugh."

McHugh gave what seems to be a rather unconvincing deposition, claiming that, in fact, all of the entertainers were amateurs. He said that the Society's investigator had met some patrons whom he knew in the saloon, and that these patrons were induced to sing, reluctantly and "without the hope or expectation of any compensation." What is more, "that such singing was not accompanied by any recitations or dialogue or any gestures, movement, or action, representing any character or expressing any emotion or passion." And further that McHugh's Free and Easy was not fitted up for any kind of theatrical performance.

The majority of shows always seem to have revolved around singing, dancing, and the usual instrumental music of various kinds (most often piano and violin). A concert saloon, after all, was a kind of music hall, first and foremost. Some songs were from popular plays of the day, especially those of Harrigan and Hart. "The Skids [the Skidmore Guards] Are Out Today," taken from their *The Mulligan Guard's Chowder,* with appropriate marching, was a great favorite in concert saloons in the seventies and eighties, and their "A Little Pitcher of Beer" was also frequently performed. In concert saloons patronized primarily by men of German birth or first-generation German-Americans – and, indeed, there were a number of such concert saloons – well-known operas were popular in the seventies, probably influenced by the beer gardens that also catered to the German community of New York.

By the eighties, increasingly, musical numbers were listed in Society reports by title, although whether this was by accident or a matter of policy is not very clear. Purely instrumental pieces also occurred more often between the acts. Orchestras appeared more frequently than in previous years; perhaps there were more musicians available, or perhaps audiences now expected orchestras. Typically, the format for such a show called for a piano number (or an orchestral selection where there was an orchestra) between the various turns. At Phelps, 50 and 52 West Thirty-first Street, in 1880, for example, a pianist "played airs in the intervals between the songs." And at The Brighton (apparently a family place) in 1881 a document noted "Numerous musical selections, by said orchestra, in the intervals following each of the performances hereinafter mentioned." There were orchestras with at least three or four instruments in perhaps a third of the concert saloons mentioned by the Society during the early eighties and most seemed to own a piano.

Dance numbers were also common. Some had sexual overtones, but they are not described in any detail. The very presence of dance without a license, however, was enough for a citation. Among the many dance routines was

one at The Newport, 502 Sixth Avenue, in 1879: "Three comic songs by
said minstrel O'Neill – and also a song and dance by said O'Neill – piano
accompaniment by same pianist [as the one who performed for the rest
of the show]." Many dance numbers seem to have had their origin on the
minstrel stage: at the end of an unidentified comic song at the Newport in the
same year, an entertainer "danced a jig and walked around." Entertainers
sang, danced, and played musical instruments, and often presented non-
musical material – usually simple rhymes or couplets – as part of their acts.
Increasingly, a number included more overtly theatrical material, in addition
to the songs themselves.

Some of the concert saloons, like Maier's Essex Hall, 170 Essex Street,
undoubtedly involved female entertainers in some acts, many of them relatively mild leg-show routines. In 1875, Maier, among other attractions,
presented, for example, "a certain dramatic performance enacted by an actress dressed in the costume of a flower girl, and carrying a basket of flowers
on her arm, who strode up and down the stage, struck various stage attitudes,
recited dialogue, and sung appropriate songs, at the same time distributing
flowers to the audience."[7] It is not known what the "dialogue" was: probably
it was simply romantic verse of some kind, addressed more or less to the
audience. Females were part of many shows after the war, and at a number
of concert saloons there were often several women performing as "minstrels"
or in leg-show acts. Female performers were finding a more or less secure
home in the concert saloons, perhaps drawn by the money, the breakdown
in some quarters of old prejudices, and the chance – infrequent at best in
the years after the Civil War – to demonstrate their talent and looks for
audiences. In some cases, as we shall see, there was little or no option for
them.

A few concert saloons featured both men and women performing together. The Garden, 45 Great Jones Street, offered a song by a woman, with
piano accompaniment, in the course of which a male performer joined in.
At the Casino, 51 Bowery, in 1883 there was "a dramatic performance including songs, dances and recitations by a Male and Female dressed in costume." Children also performed, often as singers. Among them was "Master
Devlin," whose appearance was advertised at Levy's Concert Saloon, 586
Eighth Avenue, in 1883. He may have appeared in one of the "midget minstrel" routines commonly performed by child actors at the time. Essentially
a novelty, midget-minstrel acts were versions of the kind of thing presented
by grown-up males. (In amateur minstrely, midget-minstrel routines lasted
until the middle of the twentieth century.)

Proprietors also presented other kinds of acts that were patently illegal, but which customers were happy to see for little or no money as they drank their beer. Occasionally, perhaps to the horror of those few reformers who understood the subtext, some of the routines were men impersonating women. But this sort of "drag" was common in professional minstrel shows, and these acts may have been seen as rather ordinary blackface minstrel impersonations of women. We simply do not know. We are not told by the investigators. The very existence of "performance" (whatever that was) without a license, however, was reason enough for a citation by the Society, In any case, in 1876, the Centennial Gardens, 183 Chatham Street, offered "Minstrelsy and Can Can dancing by an actor dressed in the costume of a female – short fancy dress exposing legs, white stockings." At Clinton Garden, 126–128 Clinton Street, in 1877, there was a female impersonator of some sort.

A number of entertainers from the minstrel theatres introduced blackface songs, sketches, and other acts. Minstrelsy had fallen on hard times in New York after the war, and presumably many minstrel men were glad to find work in concert saloons. It was little trouble; the performers were probably already quite familiar with the material, having presented it or at least seen it, many times.

At The Bowery Music Hall, 20 Bowery, in 1879, for example, four "negro minstrels" [as white men in blackface were called in Society reports] sang and played the banjo, bones, violin, and tambourine. Among other things, they sang as a quartet, "besides singing, marked time with their feet, shouted, and the bones and tambourine players did many ludicrous things to amuse the audience." At the Newport, a professional named Tennnyson sang a minstrel song. "At intervals during said song he addressed the audience, clapped his hands, gesticulated, and marched up and down the room. Said minstrel sang and spoke in a negro dialect." Indeed, minstrelsy – with a large number of unemployed performers in the eighties – seems to have provided the basis around which concert-saloon shows were built.

In 1881 another minstrel group presented "numerous negro minstrel songs, solos, and choruses, sung and performed on various musical instruments, among them the banjo, bones, guitar and violin cello." At Phelps, the previous year, audiences encountered a "Negro plantation Song by a negro minstrel who was accompanied on the piano – Comic Song and character sketch by another negro minstrel, who enacted in song and action a negro 'swell,' twirled a walking cane and strode up and down." Another minstrel impersonated an aged black man. At Windsor Gardens, 120 West

Fourteenth Street, in 1881, a third minstrel wore a costume that included a wig, hat, and spectacles, imitated "in accent and gesture an old negro," and performed a banjo solo.

At a reasonable estimate, up to half the acts done in post-war concert saloons appear to have come directly from minstrel shows. But that estimate should not be taken as conclusive since minstrel acts also appeared in other popular forms of the day, such as the circus, and may have come by way of one of them. Then, too, after the war, the objects of satire were changing. New immigrant groups – specifically the Irish and the Germans – were appearing in New York in large numbers. They were often laborers and servants, and the Irish especially were considered slightly subhuman. Both Irish and German immigrants were beginning to be seen on the concert-saloon stage almost as frequently as imitation blacks after the war. At O'Donnell's in 1875, a show offered an actor in an Irish routine: "That said actor evidently endeavored to imitate an Irish driver, used an Irish dialect, sung a song descriptive of a car ride, danced up and down the stage and acted as if he were driving a horse." Two years later McHugh of McHugh's Free and Easy presented a "song by a minstrel who affected an Irish brogue."

German (or Dutch, as they were called) parodies were almost equally popular. At the Centennial Gardens in 1876, a minstrel performer dressed in costume to represent a "'Stage Dutchman' – that said actor assumed a Dutch dialect, sang and acted – ." At McHugh's in 1877 there was "a comic German character song by a minstrel named Rose and who is styled 'The Celebrated German Comique' and who has performed in other places of amusement in this City – That said actor spoke & sang in a German dialect and broken English."

Though blackface minstrel material was the most common in traditional concert saloons, these parodies were perhaps the most plentiful after it. And like blackface comedy, the satire came in a number of versions, most often comic songs, but sometimes in the form of jokes, monologues, or sketches, like this one at The Fashion, 501 Sixth Avenue, in 1881: "Burlesque of an Irishman who was supposed to be attending a wake during which he contorted his features, strode up and down the room, and addressed the audience in an Irish brogue." Concert-saloon spectators could also see a "Comic song and German character sketch by a . . . minstrel, whose name is not known to deponent – Said minstrel imitated a German Soldier, marched up and down shouldering a cane for a musket and marking time with his feet."

This casual stereotyping was expected and enjoyed at concert saloons, and some satire of Jews also took place, although the great wave of Jewish immigration was to take place later. At Batchelors Music Hall, Andrew Myers, "the greatest of all character impersonators," appeared in some of his "Hebrew songs and funny sayings." At The Fashion in 1880 there was a "Song with burlesque of a Jew, during which said Busch [Frank Busch, an entertainer] wore a false beard, a pair of spectacles and a very small white hat, and had his coat collar turned up. He sang and recited humorous pieces in broken English, stroked his beard at intervals, spat on the floor, gesticulated and strode up and down the floor." Later, Busch did several other imitations, "including one of an old maid in which latter he wore a blonde wig and a pair of spectacles." A send-up of the Chinese was seen at Clinton Garden in 1877. A performer there "sang in imitation of a chinaman," though not much Chinese stereotyping appeared in Eastern concert saloons.

Gymnastic acts of all kinds often reappeared in concert saloons. But they were illegal, too, in the eyes of investigators. Even if they contained no dialogue, they were clearly in the hands of the despised professionals. In 1879 the Mabille Palace, 59 Bleecker, was cited for "numerous acrobatic performances and feats of contortion by a professional acrobat. While performing said acrobat played the bones." On the other hand, amusements that were not strictly speaking performances, such as boxing matches, almost certainly gained currency during the first days after the Concert Bill, because they were rumored, like music, to be unobjectionable to the City and the Society when not presented by obvious professionals. Exhibition boxing matches (some between blacks and whites) seem to have been fairly common. At "Ownie" Geohagan's Old House at Home, 105 Bowery, several matches were held in 1881. A wrestling exhibition took place in the same year, and there was a benefit for the two whites. In a deposition, Geohagan, trying hard to avoid a fine and imprisonment, said about the benefit wrestling match that it was "to help the families [of the contestants] who were destitute."

One act that appeared at Maier's Essex Hall, 170 Essex Street, in 1875, was obviously illegal, so far as the investigator was concerned. The routine, he said, fell under the 1872 bill – and hence the scrutiny of the Society – since it contained dialogue and song and appeared in premises that had no license to present shows. Although the act was a puppet show, and not specifically mentioned as illegal by either the 1862 or 1872 bills, its failing was that it was "exhibited by a ventriloquist, who recited dialogue, and sung in various assumed voices. [He] caused the figures used therein to go through the maneuvers on a raised platform, said entertainment being what is commonly known as a Punch and Judy show."

And there is a reference to a magic act at the Brighton in 1880, an extended description of "performances of juggling and slight of hand by a juggler [magician] who was assisted at times by a man who stood on the stage behind." The magician's performance "consisted of numerous tricks with tin cones, glasses, imitation eggs, handkerchiefs, a high black silk hat, dolls, small trunks, waggons, rolls of paper, a gold finger ring, a pack of playing cards and candles and confections." The feats, said the report, "were so performed as to deceive the spectators. One of said performances which is known as the 'Hat Trick' consisted of taking numerous articles out of an apparently empty hat and is a well-known conjuring trick and deponent has seen it performed by numerous other jugglers. At intervals during said feats there were selections on the piano by said pianist." During the performance, the investigator noted, "said juggler used a wand or stick such as is usually used by magicians, and previous to each performance he explained to the audience the nature of each trick he was about to perform. He frequently made use of the expression 'presto, change'."[8]

Thus, in addition to music, then, there were many kinds of acts, either borrowed directly from variety theatres or the minstrel show, or from other forms of popular entertainment such as the circus. It should be emphasized that comedy and gymnastic acts apparently found their way into a number of concert saloons. An example of a form that returned – or possibly never left some New York institutions – is the sketch or short play. Possibly it was sometimes an excerpt from a full-length drama or a popular comedy.

An increasing number of different acts thus began to appear, including some sketches for which we have titles, among them "Duffy's Opening Night," which played at Elwist's, 461 Sixth Avenue, in 1880, and "Stage Struck" at Myer's Concert Hall, 15 Stanton Street, in 1882, and a few obvious knock-offs from popular plays. Included in a "dramatic and minstrel performance," at the Star and Garter, 504 Sixth Avenue, in 1880, for example, was part of Harrigan and Hart's play "The Mulligan Guard's Christmas," which was at the same time being performed at the "Theatre Comique" in New York.

We hear in more detail of a sketch done at O'Donnell's in 1875: "A certain dramatic performance of farce in one act performed by actors dressed in costume adapted to the character of the piece, one carrying an imitation musket and the other a sword, who represented parts or characters in said performance peculiar thereto." About the sketch, the informant continued, "that in the course of said piece said actors recited dialogue, sung, shouted, marched up and down the stage, keeping time with music played by the orchestra, executing various military maneuvers, and indulged in many ludicrous demonstrations." (It is possible that the popular sketch may well have originated in the blackface minstrel halls and, like much minstrel material, was a satire of blacks in the military during the Civil War. Or it may have been a satire on the many Germans who fled to America to escape conscription in the nineteenth century. Or it may simply have been a fragment of a Harrigan and Hart play or some other pirated work. In any case, the sketch seemingly was a "standard" and appeared in various forms in a number of concert saloons.)

Another sketch is described the next year at the Academy of Fun. It might also have come from the blackface minstrel show. At the Academy, there took place, the investigator said, a "dramatic performance or farce in one act performed by actors, two of whom were attired in costume so as to represent negroes. That said actors danced, sung, turned somersets & indulged in many ludicrous demonstrations to amuse the audience."

The crude sketches were constantly adjusted to comment on a current play or literary work, or a ridiculous political situation. Their origins, like most oral-tradition works, often remain somewhat obscure. And at the distance of more than a century and a quarter, it is not always easy to distinguish what was in fact a sketch. But it seems clear that some were almost what we would term one-act plays today; others consisted of little more than an extended joke – the "premise," as it was usually called in later burlesque. Often, a few lines generally led up to the climax, with the performers improvising most of the dialogue and adding their own material. Many sketches provided the excuse for introducing "business" known to the performers and more or less appropriate to the sketch being performed. (Conversely, a number of the so-called premises of sketches were to become the starting point for a monologue, song, or dance.)

In any event, as the old San Francisco performer Dora Barrett points out, the sketches were always important cultural documents and were always being reshaped to fit current situations. "Sometimes," she says, "[they were] a forum for the social ills of the day. Political content or criticism was treated handily in humor or satire. At times they satirized popular plays of the day, as when MacIntyre and Heath, the blackened twosome, became famous for 'The Worst Born,' their satirization of Francis J. Powers 'The First Born.' I regret these skits are a lost art."[9]

Barrett remembers that, at the turn of the century, everyone on the bill at a concert saloon knew a version of the same sketches (which were probably called "afterpieces" no matter when they appeared because of their relationship to the final part of some minstrel shows). In the case of a typical sketch, the familiar "Irish Justice," for example, one performer might take the role of the bailiff, another the justice, a third, the old lady who beat the dog, and a fourth, the policeman. Then they would improvise around their roles and the basic story. The sketches were almost usually more or less ad-libbed, with traditional jokes and business interpolated into the basic story.

The "premise," as Barrett says, is that a man is arrested for drunkenness. Throughout the skit, the drunken defendant and the Irish Justice keep sharing a jug of liquor that is supposed to be in evidence. "Once when I played in this skit," she writes, "I was a boy brought in, accused of having stolen a loaf of bread. The Irish Justice gave me 'life'; then, when he wasn't looking, I reached up and stole the ink well. I was caught in this dastardly act and the Justice sentenced me to ten years more ... "[10]

Many of the sketches, of course, were frankly racist, though there was little understanding at the time of the implications of racism. Stereotypes about race, ethnicity, gender, or handicaps were seen by most audience members as universal and quite funny. Women, of course, were always targets, as they were always to be in later forms of popular entertainment.

Like the famous Italian commedia dell'arte before it, the improvised comedy in America undoubtedly called for a kind of rehearsal very different from that seen in the modern legitimate theatre. The performers at a concert saloon probably knew the outlines of the agreed-upon sketch, as well as a store of jokes and physical comedy that could be inserted at will. As a result, everyone probably ad-libbed until the various versions were more or less reconciled in rehearsal. (In a medicine show – another of the many forms of popular entertainment in which concert-saloon performers took part – this kind of rehearsal process was simply, but significantly, known as "talking it over.") Since the premise and bits were so well known, perhaps, if there was no time for rehearsal, the entertainers simply went straight to performance. Because they moved so frequently between forms, memorizing material wherever they went, this kind of unrehearsed performance made perfect sense to most of them.

Examples from Society documents created between November of 1876 and May of 1877 suggest a fairly typical concert-saloon entertainment some dozen years after the end of the Civil War, when waiter girls were a novelty that was dying out. Carroll's Sixth Avenue Saloon was located on the ground floor at 455 Sixth Avenue. The owner was one Thomas Carroll and his saloon's offerings were, as various reports pointed out, advertised on placards in the window. His saloon was, the reports said, fitted up in the usual manner of such places. As the Society's form read, the establishment was "adapted to the exhibition of performances of minstrelsy, parts in Opera, and other entertainments of the stage, the rear portion there being set apart for and devoted to, the exhibition of performances hereinafter mentioned; piano, seats arranged for spectators, and such other arrangements as are usual in Concert-Rooms and places where minstrelsy and other public performances of the character above specified, are exhibited."[11]

On one of the evenings in question in the winter of 1876, "deponent [an investigator hired by the Society] saw exhibited to the public, in said concert-room, certain entertainments of the stage, consisting of performances of minstrelsy." Some fifty to a hundred spectators were in attendance during the performances, and the owner acted as manager and master of ceremonies. "Each of said performances was announced by the manager [who was probably Carroll himself], who called out the name of each person who was about to appear." (This made the added expense of programs unnecessary, and seems to have been fairly commonplace in concert saloons.) All the investigators in 1876 and 1877 were apparently satisfied that paid professionals, rather than unpaid volunteers, appeared onstage during the various performances.

The shows during the period when the Society investigated Carroll's were similar, though the acts were not always presented in the same order. And apparently, sometimes, they contained new material. Typically, Carroll's entertainment usually began with a solo or duet, often to the accompaniment of a banjo and a piano played by a blind man. Next there frequently came a song called "Stand By Your Friend." Then there sometimes appeared a banjoist – Horace Westen, who will be discussed later – and another minstrel, Edward Burton. (The banjo player and the pianist apparently appeared regularly at Carroll's; perhaps the other performers did not. In fact, the perfomers may have been hired catch-as-catch-can to fill in with their own specialties.)

After this opening often another act appeared. It was "descriptive of an Irish Jaunting Car ride sung by an actor or minstrel, who accompanied his singing by gestures, and who effected an Irish brogue." On one evening, another act was described more fully, as "minstrelsy and character acting, by an actor who represented an old man and who wore an old high black hat, spectacles, his coat collar turned up, and a handkerchief around his neck on the outside of said collar. That said actor had also a heavy cane upon which he leaned as if for support – That, at times, said actor tottered up and down said room in imitation of an old and feeble man."[12] The subsequent act, which appeared some evenings but not others, was a blackface minstrel number that employed piano, banjo, bones and tambourine.

Sometimes the brief program ended with a piano solo by the blind performer or another song with "piano accompaniment, by an actor who put on an old, damaged [white] silk hat, which had been lying on top of the piano, buttoned up his coat collar, and marched up and down." (Perhaps this was only the earlier routine transferred to the end.) In any case, occasionally this was preceded by a recitation. Songs in the show mentioned in several reports included "There's a Letter in the Candle" and "My Son Charlie." There were sometimes as few as three acts and sometimes as many as eight – probably depending on the talents and inclinations of those performers who were available and the size of the owners purse at the time. Entertainment, after all, was an advertising device, a "loss leader," which the owner or manager felt should – like the waiter girls – bring customers into his establishment and help him to sell more alcohol, and perhaps prostitutes as well. Acts were, in effect, part of the advertising budget.

A survey of the acts seen at Levy's Concert Room, on Friday, September 28, 1883, suggests the typical offerings in a second low-end concert saloon. Levy's, the report reads, had a "raised stage [perhaps merely a simple platform] and piano on the same." In the concert room the Society's investigator saw "certain entertainments of the stage as follows:

Piano and bones playing by two male performers.
Song by a male performer, piano accompaniment.
Piano and bones playing by two male performers.
Song by a male performer, piano accompaniment, known as Dan Weaver.
Comic song by a performer known as Charles Ladendorfer, piano accompaniment.
Piano and bones playing by two male performers.
Another song by the said Charles Ladendorfer, piano accompaniment."

A Poster bearing the following inscription in a window of said Concert Room.

Grand Concert given this evening by the following artists, James Butler, the only correct imitator of J. K. Emmet [a prominent minstrel performer] assisted by the renowned comic singer Charles Ladendorfer with the popular tenor singer Master Devlin and the Old War Horse with his plantation songs and imitations. William Brand, accompanied by the distinguished piano player Charles Walters. Also the Champion Bones Player Dan Weaver.

The show was apparently all male and constructed around minstrel acts, many of them featuring songs. The situation at Levy's underlines the assumption that the saloons were disposed to take the acts that already were known to managers and were available, and to build their shows around them as it was economically feasible to do so. That Levy's focused around minstrel material is scarcely surprising. As indicated earlier, by the eighties minstrelsy itself had been immensely popular and toward the end of the nineteenth century was on the decline in New York, throwing many performers out of work in the minstrel halls and undoubtedly pushing a large number into the concert saloons. Minstrel routines, however, were not the only ones in concert saloons. There were always others, drawn from various corners of popular entertainment – the circus, say, or dime museums. Undoubtedly, there also were variety theatre performers, of course.

The post-Civil War period was to see the growth of a new kind of "family" concert saloon in New York, but the traditional male-oriented concert saloon hung on. At first, some owners and managers were cautious enough to play by what they imagined were Albany's rules, however amorphous. At the same time, some obviously felt safe enough to add new kinds of – patently illegal – acts. A number of concert saloons indeed probably escaped prosecution, for whatever reasons. That post-war Society documents exist at all, however, testifies to the fact that a few of the remaining concert saloons were unlucky or unwise enough to fall foul of the various bills. After the war, waiter girls were giving way to male waiters, but prosecutions were increasing based on the fact that an institution – of whatever kind – had not paid for a proper license. Some of the places cited by the Society in the seventies and eighties were undoubtedly traditional concert saloons – probably largely sans waiter girls. Some were other institutions of quite a different sort.

4

Concert saloons: spaces and equipment

That the interior of said concert room was fitted up in a manner adapted to
the exhibition of dramatic performances, minstrelsy, parts in plays, and other
entertainments of the stage.

From the Society's standard investigative form for concert saloons

AT FIRST, OWNERS AND MANAGERS OF CONCERT SALOONS
kept their heads down. Establishments operating after the Concert Bill
seem increasingly to have moved into cellars, probably in part to seem
unobtrusive – though, of course, many had always sought out cheap quarters,
often basements or upper floors in a building with an entertainment connection. The use of basements was so common that concert saloons were
spoken of generally as housed in cellars. Of course, they were not always,
although many were indeed "Below the Sidewalk." Ballard's What Is It, for
example, occupied the basement of a building that also housed a gymnasium
and a billiard hall. Previously, it had been the home of a menagerie. (The
original What Is It?, by the way, was William Henry Johnson, a professional
"freak" and the most popular attraction in nineteenth-century America.)

Post-1862 concert saloons were cautious as well as thrifty. Presumably
owners and managers felt that, until the heat was off totally, they might
be left alone – and remain popular with male customers – if they were
in out-of-the-way, amusement-oriented places. Most inhabited slightly
raffish quarters in, or in close proximity to, New York City's entertainment districts. Perhaps concert saloons also were limited in some way in
their choice of neighborhoods, and perhaps they were obliged to make a
financial contribution to those in control as "insurance" against arrest or
the wrong kind of notoriety. (It was, after all, a time and place of considerable civic corruption.) Or perhaps they simply hoped against hope

that they would not be discovered by the wrong people and be fined or imprisoned.

Yet, in some kind of spirit of mild defiance, some concert saloons advertised their location and their wares in newspapers (the *Herald* was a favorite), or in handbills distributed on the street or inside the saloon. An 1881 report on the Bremer Haven reads "Schedule A hereto annexed is a hand bill that was given to deponent by a man stationed at the entrance to said place who was distributing copies of the bill to passers by." The Bremer Haven handbill announced free admission, both in English and German, and continued in English, stating the fact that there was a "Banjo Concert and Singing" inside, as well as giving the address of the saloon and the fact that "FRESH LAGER" was available at five cents a glass.

Most handbills and posters that investigators saw were general advertising for the concert saloon itself. At the Bremer Haven, in 1881, for example, we are told that there was "a sign at the entrance to said concert room [that] bore the following inscription, 'Bremer Haven Saloon. Musical and Vocal entertainments every evening. Admission free -.'" A few traditional concert saloons, however, made a point in handbills or posters stating the fact that they were featuring a star or an unusual act. Thus, in 1880, Elvists' placed a notice in a window to attract audiences to a special event, the appearance of Horace Westen and Tom Butler. A sign-board bearing another notice stood on the Street near the entrance to the concert room: "Free concert every evening. List of talent. Horace Weston [*sic*], accompanied by Tom Butler, Johnny Roach." Signs on sandwich boards worn by men hired by the managers were also in common use, the investigators said.

Glaring transparencies like those often used by some dime museums were a much employed, and often maligned, feature of concert-saloon advertising. A journalist named Podhammer investigated concert saloons for the *Home Journal*. He wrote dismissively in May, 1857, about "a concert saloon on the Bowery" at which there was a huge "transparency, which read: 'Musical Hall – Free Concert Every Evening – Sacred Music on Sunday Evening.'" (Like the signs inside that asked patrons not to applaud on Sunday evenings, signs like these were an obvious and often-used way to get around New York's famous Blue Law, which prohibited secular Sunday shows.)

Spread across windows among the posters and placards, or on fronts of buildings, the transparencies were made of canvas or muslin, stretched on frames and lighted from behind. About the one at the Melodeon, an 1864 article in the *Clipper* says, "The exterior is very showy, having three conspicuous transparencies, notifying the citizens, furloughed soldiers, officers of the navy, and returned volunteers that it is 'the best place of its kind in New York.' 'Free to all,' says the handwriting on the canvas. 'George Haydon's Great Opera, Free and Easy Every Evening,' with other extra novelties, 'to be seen in no other concert hall in the city.'"[1] At The Academy of Fun in 1876 the unique charms of the place were advertised both "by illuminated transparencies & large colored placards stationed in front of the concert room." Many other concert saloons advertised their special attractions in a similarly flamboyant way.

Some writers disagreed with the majority opinion and found a number of the transparencies tastefully done. Concert saloons like the New Oriental on Broadway, were "theme" establishments, with the theme carried out – in spite of the polyglot show inside – in the costumes of the waiter girls, in the decor, and of course, on the facade. At the New Oriental, said the *Clipper*, there were "splendiferous" pictures outside. One was an arched, illuminated canvas about ten feet square, "a capitally executed painting done in oil, of a Turkish *couchant*... with her servant holding over her alabaster neck a sunshade, and at the foot of the stairs [leading down to the concert saloon] another Turkess ... These transparencies are no gingerbread affairs, but gems of the banner painter's art."[2]

Blatant gas signs (sometimes electric in later years) were seen on the facades of some concert saloons, and in the interiors of a few. They were a novelty much commented on in the press. At the Star and Garter, in 1879, for example, a report said "That the words 'Star and Garter' in lighted gas jets were placed in a conspicuous position in said concert room." At Ownie Geohagan's place, two years later, we are told that "the words (in gold letters) 'Geohagan, Manager' appeared in one of the street windows of said concert room, and a large electric light blazed above the door." Ballard's What Is It, the *Clipper* said, had a transparency of the popular freak Zeke, the What Is It?. There was also, the article continued, a "revolving light of many colors" over the front door, "cunningly devised, wheels within wheels, which, when in working order, is very showy. It is moved by clock-work; but it hasn't been going the rounds lately, owing to some disarrangement in its internals."

A photograph in the Museum of the City of New York (probably taken around the turn of the century) shows the exterior of a late concert saloon, the Lyceum Concert Garden at 302 Bowery. It was a modest first-floor establishment much like an ordinary shop. There was a cheap hotel above that offered rooms – or at least beds – for fifteen and twenty cents a night. The signs for both the hotel and the concert saloon are outlined in light bulbs, apparently turned on during the day. Admission to the concert saloon is free, and the facade is plastered with banners and window cards advertising the Curtis and Heath Minstrel Burlesque Company. The company featured a "Grand Cake Walk," as well as, "Extra This Week," some sort of added act or other attraction (the card is unreadable), and free matinees. Whether the matinees were now aimed at men and women or women and children is not made clear.

Admission to some concert saloons (especially the grander ones) was not always free. Sometimes – particularly when there was a special event – there was a kind of cover charge. Twenty-five cents was typical for those that *did* charge. When admission was indeed free, ten or fifteen cents usually had to be spent on drinks by patrons. Some early concert saloons, on the other hand, charged admission fees for a so-called "private box" that ranged from thirteen cents to fifty cents – perhaps with a prostitute in attendance. To avoid trouble, a few concert saloons, even before the Concert Bill, made clear that "we admit no boys."

Some of the classic concert saloons used programs. But not many have survived as attachments to Society documents, and most seem not to have used them. A few of the later family-oriented saloons in New York that gave shows did, however, offer spectators programs much like those given out by variety theatres. Typically they contained, along with a program of the show, advertisements and jokes that bore no relationship to the entertainment being given that night. In 1880, in the "Brighton Gazette," a program of a family-oriented concert saloon known as the Brighton Winter Garden, for example, there were ancient jokes like this one: "A laborer of Hibernian extraction was not long since lamenting the hard times and said finally, 'av I was only back in me father's palace'. A jolly fellow workman squinted his eye, and replied: 'Sure, an' av ye wore there, ye might sthan' an the groun' and reach yer han' down the chimbley an' open the door av it.'"3

Concert-saloon entertainments, for the most part, appear to have been adjuncts to conventional saloons. The famous screen at the Bon Ton, in fact, served a practical function. It separated the bar from the show and the waiter girls, and masked what were obvious illegal activities from the street. But it also had another use. "As neither boys nor drunken soldiers," the *Clipper* said, "are tolerated except in the bar-room, and only when they behave themselves, no chance is afforded here to those disposed to be dishonest of being tempted to do what they would be sorry for afterwards."4 Only "respectable" clientele, said the *Clipper*, were allowed behind the screen at the Bon Ton. (This, of course, implies that the less-than-respectable were kept in front of it. Just how this was determined is not clear; critics would say that it was *not* determined.)

In some cases – nobody knows how many – concert saloons were not too different from conventional small theatres and variety houses, with more or less proper stages and auditoriums, usually small ones, sometimes with a floor that sloped in the direction of the stage in order to provide spectators with better sight lines. In such houses audience seats were made with a rack or shelf on the back for drinks. About the Novelty, 616 Broadway, we hear that it was a rather long, narrow room, with a raised bar at the back, so that drinkers standing at the back of the house could watch the show over the heads of spectators. The walls of the room were covered with paper in some sort of theatrical pattern and the stage held only a single set, used for all acts. The rows of seats accommodated "a sort of wooden gutter to hold the drinking utensils."

But concert saloons came in every size and shape, as well as every sort and condition. Characteristically, once inside, the reveler typically was confronted by a place not too different from a conventional saloon, a long room with flat floor and tables and chairs. A more or less typical small establishment was The Gaieties, described in an unnamed clipping in the Harvard Theatre Collection. It featured "a bar, a long room with a low ceiling, its walls decorated with pictures of Heenan, Bill Poole, Titian's Venus and bills proclaiming the prices of the drinks retailed, a sanded floor, tables, chairs . . ." It also contained "a stage, with a gaily-painted set scene (probably intended for a view of Constantinople), a piano, a violin, and an average number of frequenters and waiter-girls."

On the Bowery, Podhammer saw a concert saloon in a large room on the third floor of a building, "furnished with long rows of tables and chairs, a bar at one end, and a stage at the other." By contrast, the Novelty appears to have been remodeled from some sort of theatre space (a not uncommon occurrence). There were ordinary boxes, so-called "private boxes," an orchestra, and a gallery. Admission was thirteen cents to ordinary boxes, a quarter to the orchestra, and fifty cents to the so-called private boxes.

But the floor of most concert saloons typically was flat, to accommodate tables and chairs, not raked as in a proper theatre. In any event, the majority drew no more than seventy-five or a hundred spectators – sometimes fewer – and were not capable of seating more than a couple of hundred. There were exceptions, of course. The *Clipper* points to the Reveille, 594 Broadway, as "immense," and says that the "capacity will fairly astonish you." There was, the paper writes, an extensive broad bar counter, and behind that another wide sideboard with everything at the bartender's hands. No ranges of fancy painted bottles or frivolous signs; everything looks like business. To the left were two large tables with snowy table covers in case some of the visitors should wish a dejuner of fricasseed frogs or boned turkey, same style as usual. Near these tables stood several fancy velvet-backed chairs, same style as used at our fashionable theatres. Several very fine steel engravings and oil paintings ornament the walls. The bar-room proper is about eighty feet in length, and twenty in width, nicely oilclothed and papered . . . The grand salon is about 120 feet in length, making the entire extent equal to 200 feet in length, running through from Broadway to Crosby Street [below Houston] . . . In the lower room there are forty large, round tables, and on each table a set of dominoes (most everybody can play at dominoes) . . . In the for'ard part, as sailors have it, the proprietor, Mr. Simpson . . . has an office.[5]

The *Clipper* claimed that there were "no private rooms or anything objectionable" in the Reveille. Indeed, the place supposedly employed two deputy sheriffs to prevent "boisterous talking or loud arguments."

Some concert saloons inhabited unusually elaborate spaces. The New Oriental, for example, the *Clipper* claimed, had a "gorgeous" interior, "fairly dazzling to the eyes." "The illuminated walls, parti-colored cut-paper ceiling ornaments, brilliant gaslights and the pretty waiter girls flitting up and down in their variegated costumes made us think we had been transported (not by the government, but at our own individual expense) into fairyland, like Aladdin and his wonderful lamp."[6]

Other concert saloons were relatively modest. About the interior of the Occidental the *Clipper* says:

The room is not a very extensive one, but [the proprietor, William Allen], if he and the tax gatherers come to terms and he gets a new lease on life under the curb, has a design in his head to knock down the old partition and run his saloon away back into Mercer Street [below Houston Street]. At present the place is not as showy as some other saloons we've seen, yet everything is comfortable; and with a good hot stove, a little bourbon, and "that young gal dressed in blue" alongside, people must be hard to please if under these circumstances they are not as happy as a clam at high tide.[7]

In most concert saloons of whatever quality there was a bar at the side, or near the entrance, or in another room, and sometimes private dining rooms, which were simply what the name implied, not places for prostitution or assignations. Of the bar at Lee and Hatstatt's Eureka, at 554 Broadway (not to be confused with Shafer's concert saloon of the same name at Broadway and Spring), the *Clipper* said in 1864: "[the bar] is where champagne bottles [are] done up so snug and neat that it seems a pity to draw the corks. They were ranged like miniature grenadiers, and all other kinds of liquids from 'dead beat' to 'Heidsick' were found." The article continued,

> on one side of the bar, hung a gold 'ticker' to be raffled for . . . Above the 'ticker' dangled a notice to the effect that no tick was allowed there; and then again above that the old, played out motto: 'No money loaned less than $1,000,' from which we are led to suppose that concert saloon people must be invested by those 'on the borrow' more than most folk. The next 'ornament' was a revolver, hung there probably as a 'persuader' to keep the roughs and lovers from raising fusses, assaulting waiters, and such like innocent pastimes of the Seven Dials' breed. We can't say, however, that we like to see a loaded blunderbuss displayed so conspicuously, looking as it does like somebody's death warrant.[8]

Cheap popular pictures seem to have existed on the walls of most concert saloons; often these were either "sporting" or "theatrical" prints, two favorites of patrons. But the *Clipper* said that in 1864 Lee and Hatstatt's Eureka featured "pictures of ships and scenery . . . hung high enough to prevent meddlesome fellows from handling and mauling them about. Circus bills and menagerie bills and bills of various other kinds are festooned around the bar." Shafer's Eureka, the paper said, in the same article, possessed "four or five pictures of hunting and fishing scenes."

Many of the pictures, of course, were considered provocative at the time. At the Occidental, for example, we are told by the *Clipper* reporter, there was "a painting of Nell Gwynne (or someone else) dressed somewhat like Mazeppa undressed, just after performing the great bareback act. A little further on is the picture of a young lady with nothing to wear, laying off in an 'easy' position; and between the two, a third female with 'overalls' on."[9] The reporter for the *Clipper* tells us that these pictures had formerly been at another concert saloon, and promises others of a like nature, "only a little more so," in the future.

George Haydon's Melodeon substituted pictures painted directly on the walls. At the Melodeon, one passed behind a screen of some kind and entered the main room. "On the walls are painted the figures of two females in very gaudy costumes, with dresses short at both ends, and a pair of understandings worthy of Vestris." In the inner space, there was a picture

of the ubiquitous comic Irishman. "Between the two fair ladies is a gentleman fresh from Iniskillen, with his sprig of shillelelagh [*sic*] and shamrock so green, ready for a ruction or Lannegan's ball, no matter which."
Elsewhere on the walls there were designs and some important information. "The other portions of the wall are ornamented with little fillamagrees
and jimcracks, curious designs, which none but the artist can properly explain. In the center of the room forming a sort of terrestrial canopy, is
a large scroll, telling the unbenighted how much to pay for wine by the
pint or quart on one side, with figures of naked nymphs dancing . . . on the
other."[10]

The "sideboard" appears in a number of concert saloons, and undoubtedly
contained a "free lunch" available to customers, like that at most neighborhood saloons. At Presto Hall in 1864, the *Clipper* says, was "a table
loaded down with bologna, sandwiches, ham, sardines, corned beef, etc.,
with a dozen different kinds of pickles. Behind the table is a plate rack,
"surmounted by a picture of a lion's head with three or four ears of corn in
his mouth, and the words 'Speyers and Bernheimer's Lager Beer' painted
on it."

It may have been true that most places where the Society sent an observer
or observers contained some kind of theatre space. At least the Society
claimed that theatre spaces were present, and had the assertion printed on
all of the forms used for its reports. Depositions made by owners attempting
to avoid the fines, however, usually omitted any reference to theatre spaces,
but the depositions *do* give a good general picture of the interiors of their
concert saloons. An owner named Maier is quite detailed about the contents
of his saloon but never speaks about a stage and theatrical equipment being
present:

> I rent the saloon and three rooms above it in the same house . . . I own the
> furniture in the room. I own the fixtures. There is a counter in the saloon
> which I own and about sixty or eighty chairs. The bar in the place is fitted
> up and supplied with the necessary glasses, bottles, &c. to conduct the
> business of selling lager beer, weiss beer, soda water, &c. I own the piano
> in the saloon. I own no other musical instrument in use in the saloon. Five
> years ago the piano cost $500 . . . I can't tell how much it is worth now.
> There are two pictures on the wall, one King Gambinus and the other
> Bacchus. I know they are not oil paintings and can be bought I suppose
> for 20 cts apiece. The frames are worth about 75c each. There is a mirror
> of size about 3 × 11. feet with black walnut frame. It is cracked across.
> There are no other furniture or fixtures.[11]

At Ownie Geohegan's place, the Old House at Home, all the Society reports in 1881 referred to the investigators seeing a raised stage, sometimes with a piano on it, and a musician playing a violin. Probably the room in which the stage was located was on the second floor – at least several of the reports mention it as being there. But Geohegan conveniently forgets it in his deposition, although he provides some information about a prize ring that was undoubtedly just as damaging as far as the City and the Society were concerned. "The first floor of said premises," he says, "is a room about forty feet long by twenty feet wide ... it contains a bar for refreshments, chairs, tables and benches for the accommodation of visitors":

> About the middle of the room is a raised platform, a foot and a half from the ground, commonly called a twenty four foot ring, and at the corner of the room is an old instrument called a piano ... the interior of said barroom is not fitted up in a manner adapted to the exhibition of dramatic performances, minstrelsy, parts in opera and other amusements of the stage, but on the contrary, is fitted up as a place where lovers of the art of self defense may meet in peace and look upon the pictures of those who have become known in the annals of the prize ring, of famous boatmen, of great runners and wrestlers.[12]

After Society investigators claimed, on rather scanty evidence, that he put on shows, William Schwab, the owner of an apparently family-oriented concert saloon at 2387 Third Avenue, deposed in 1884 that he did not permit "performances," and described his establishment as simply a "beer garden, saloon and restaurant." Indeed, this fact was also confirmed by the depositions of his employees. He and his workers may well have been telling the truth, and perhaps Schwab was simply a prospect for a fine in a period when fines seem to have been declining and the Society needed the funds. At any rate, Schwab admitted that there was a stage of sorts in his saloon, but gave a non-theatrical reason for its presence. His musicians and singers were not even the reason for the platform. In his deposition, Schwab admitted as well that he employed the female musicians noted in the affidavit. But they were, he said, "neatly and plainly dressed in evening dresses, and their dresses had no more resemblance to stage costumes than the evening dress of any respectable lady."

Schwab seemingly denied little. He freely – or creatively – admitted, "That at the end of said saloon there is a raised platform," (which well may itself have been illegal and, in any case, tended to prove to the Society that illegal performances took place there). But, he maintained that the platform was chiefly "built to wind up and attend" the orchestrion, "said orchestrion being a large musical instrument worked by springs and machinery [and seemingly legal]. That said platform is about twenty inches high." Schwab went on, offering a further explanation:

> I purchased the said orchestrion about three years ago, and had steps built at the side thereof to wind it up, but owing to the fact that frequently through the carelessness of my employees in attending the same, it became disarranged and necessitated work in the front portion thereof, and the steps were of no avail for that purpose, and I was compelled to use chairs etc. in order to reach the portion thereof that was necessary to be attended to, and I therefore about eighteen months ago, built around it a low platform about twenty inches in height in order that the person attending it [might] get at any portion thereof ... in case of accident.[13]

The Society did not dispute Schwab's explanation, saying only that he had "a raised stage, and that he had an orchestrion, a piano, and an orchestra on the same." Schwab countered that he did not charge admission (neither, seemingly, did the majority of concert saloons), and that "the sole object of having the music was to endeavor to make my place a respectable and enjoyable resort." He went on: "It is not true as stated in said affidavits, and each of them, that they, the said affiants, or either of them, saw, on any occasions, in said affidavit mentioned, 'exhibited on the stage of said Concert Garden any Entertainments of the stage.'" He continued, describing his establishment:

> the room has only twenty five tables and six chairs to each table, and would not accommodate more than one hundred and fifty persons if full. That rarely if ever are there more than twenty five persons at one time in said place ... That the whole room is open on the inside from the street ... And in one room, in the front portion thereof is my bar, lunch and segar counters all placed, and in the rear is the restaurant.[14]

He persevered, countering the charges resolutely, saying that "there are no curtains, footlights, nor any paraphernalia of the stage nor anything tending, appertaining or belonging to the stage in said room."

But the Society generally noted a raised stage or a proscenium arch of any sort. And evidently a stage of any kind seemed to them to imply automatic guilt. An 1875 report from the Society on Maier's Essex Halle, for example, specifies that the room contained a stage with a "curtain, scenery, both side scenes (painted to represent foliage) and a flat (representing a background), and that a bell was rung to start the show." Often the stage was

8 Stock poster for a concert saloon, *c.* 1860

at the far end of the main room, out of sight of passers-by in the street, or sometimes in a back room, or a space walled off from the street, as at the Bon Ton. It was usually either a platform, a proscenium stage, or a proscenium with a stage behind it and a deep platform-like forestage in front. In 1876 the Centennial Garden presumably had some sort of stage (probably a proscenium) with "draperies," and the next year Clinton Garden possessed "scenery, both side scenes and a flat, representing a garden – side lights on stage." Something like this seems to have been fairly common in concert saloons.

A number of them, including the Centennial Garden, even boasted a dressing room off their stages, and in 1875, O'Donnells had "wings through which the actors entered." A report on the Brighton Winter Garden, 55 Great Jones, for example, adds "that it [the alleged concert saloon] was fitted up with a raised stage, orchestra – composed of piano, violin, and flute – on the stage." Probably, in some places, however, there was only an open space for performance, where use simply did not justify the expense of constructing a conventional proscenium and related fittings. Many owners of course who did not possess either platform or proscenium claimed – and perhaps they were right – that their saloons did *not* present performances. But this is what the Society regularly maintained.

A stock poster, probably from the Civil War era, is evidently aimed at concert saloons, however. (A hundred posters in one color cost $20.00, and in four colors, $34.00.) The poster shows a rather garish room with naked caryatids on either side of a proscenium stage with footlights. On the stage there are dancers and draperies reminiscent of those in the notorious musical play *The Black Crook*. Women, apparently waiter girls, are scurrying about with trays of drinks, and one of them is leaning provocatively on a table, at which several men are seated. A bar is in the right foreground, with the bartender mixing some elaborate concoction. Several waiter girls are picking up drinks, and some are seated with male customers.

A stage, of course, seems to call for some kind of set – especially since the Society forms conventionally spoke of buildings which were "fitted up in a manner adapted to the exhibition of dramatic performances, minstrelsy, parts in opera, and other entertainments of the stage [and contain] such other arrangements as are usual in concert rooms and places where minstrel and other public performances are exhibited."[15] For the most part, however, little detailed information exists about sets. It appears, though, that they were rather minimal in most concert saloons. Where a set existed, it was apparently more or less permanent, used for many acts, attempting not so much to set the particular scene as to provide a workable background for the performer. Such a background was common in the nineteenth century. Indeed, a similarly casual position about the function of sets in popular entertainment is seen into the early twentieth century. Thus, for example, the Toby Show, a kind of American tent show, was content to provide audiences with four utility settings, known to show people as "front room," "back room," "timber," and "town," into which almost any play would fit. And many medicine shows did with even less in the way of settings, relying on a few costume pieces and properties to set the scene. (Overall, we have even less information about lighting; it probably was fairly crude and limited in most saloons that were fitted out for performance. There were footlights at some, we know, but probably little more on most concert-saloon stages.)

The use of costume in concert saloons is a bit more complex. Some concert saloons employed what should be considered costume in some acts; others seem to have made do with the ordinary dress of the day (especially for men) and a few costume elements that sketched in a character. In any case, actors of all kinds were probably expected to provide their own wardrobes, as they did in most popular entertainments. Perhaps they could supply costumes that they had worn for their act in another popular form, re-using them for concert-saloon performances. Stage costume certainly was sometimes employed by female performers in concert saloons. At the Casino, 51 Bowery, in 1882, for example, there was a "Comic song by a female in fancy costume, and . . . flesh colored tights and fancy slippers – at the end of each she waltzed up and down the stage." But this was not all of it. She was encored and sang another song, and there was a song by "another female who was dressed in fancy costume and wore tights of a light color and fancy shoes."

Several New York City concert saloons were also reported to have a dance floor, usually an open space for dancing in front of the stage. A few (nobody knows how many, see Chapter 5) were in effect concert saloons *and* dance houses; Harry Hills is the best-known example. Also in front of the raised stage – if there was one, or in the balcony, if it existed; it did not at many concert saloons – was the area for a piano, or, in some cases, a small orchestra.

This was the situation in 1882 at Hubert's Prospect Concert Garden, at 106 and 108 Fourteenth Street, evidently a family resort. There was also "a balcony in which there was an orchestra composed of two males and five females," as well as tables and chairs for customers. But the music could be almost anywhere in the saloon where it would fit. At Lee and Hatstatt's Eureka, for example, it was stuck in the northeast corner (played by a member of the Smith family of musicians, who seem to have specialized in concert-saloon work). Often a piano was on the stage itself.

For the most part, however, many concert saloons probably did not contain the balcony shown in movies. Balconies were apparently more common in the large dance houses. The Buckingham, a dance house, for example, Mc Cabe says, contained "a gaudily decorated apartment, two stories in height, with gallery running around it on a level with the second story." But balconies were not unknown, especially in concert saloons remodeled from theatres or minstrel houses that had had a balcony in the first place. The Canterbury Music Hall, on Broadway between Houston and Prince, was certainly a converted theatre. In 1862, an article mentions a parquet stretching from the stage back to the bar, which covered the back wall of the room. An open "promenade" raised some four feet above the parquet, allowed spectators to see what was going on on-stage while buying a drink. The old theatre gallery had been fitted out with compartments, where the reporter saw the waiter girls both serving and drinking with customers.

Prostitutes reportedly sometimes plied their trade in concert-saloon balconies, or in rooms purposely set aside for sex. Sometimes the prostitutes worked in spaces decorously called "curtained boxes" when a balcony
surrounded the main floor. (Similar boxes – but simply used for seating, not
sex – existed in the English music hall and in the American "flat floor opera
house" that developed in the second half of the nineteenth century. And of
course in proper theatres. Boxes – sometimes apparently used for sex, as the
Epilogue suggests – were to appear in the American West.)

A number of concert saloons continued to be wary about anything that
could clearly be identified as "performance" – especially if females were
present and obvious to investigators. At least one concert saloon, the Opera
Saloon, had an amenity that was "entertainment" but not "performance." It
featured a billiard table. Many concert saloons routinely contained shooting
galleries, either in the main room or in a special space connected to it. In
1864, Shafer's Eureka, for example, had one at the extreme end of the hall.
"Pretty nearly all the underground ranches, have one," said the *Clipper*,
referring to the fact that many concert saloons were in basements. "And
from the way that they are patronized it would appear that the target men
do a slashing business out of their 'three shots for five pence.'" At the
Eureka, for example, there were two figures, each with a bugle, flanking a
target:

> On the right . . . sat the painting of some old commonwealth burgher,
> not unlike Oliver Cromwell, whom everyone has not seen and therefore
> cannot accuse us of misrepresenting the picture. To the left stood an
> old Dutch burgher, ready to burst, with an awfully exaggerated tin horn.
> Betwixt and between these two rapscallions were two more figures, a
> sailor and a nymph with very short linen. They had clay pipes stuck in
> various parts of their body; but for why we knoweth not.[16]

A few concert saloons boasted a Punch and Judy booth, or a resident
phrenologist. An article in the *Clipper* about the Champion Music Hall
described "a lean, cadaverous woe-begone looking personage [who] broke in
upon the scene to examine the craniums of all who desired at two shillings a
pop. This person, who resembled Dan Bryant in *Les Miserables*, was no less
a personage than Professor Wheeler, 'the phrenologist.' He felt our bumps
and Grovesteen's [the manager's] bumps and the female jig dancer's bumps
and one of the pretty waiter girl's bumps. We got an extraordinary good
character – better than we deserved; but he told the truth to the others – at
least they said so."[17]

Ballard's What Is It displayed stereoscopes (probably some form of "penny-in-the-slot" machines) down the center of the room. "Instead of 'gems for gentlemen only' and French pictures 'taken from life,'" said the *Clipper*, "the stereopticon contained views of cities, rivers, rural scenery, with here and there a fast-looking picture, but not one particle worse than a group of European theatrical celebrities on view in the broad sunlight on the most frequented part of Broadway."[18]

In an era before air conditioning, a number of concert saloons (both classic male-oriented ones and those that catered to families) had attached or adjacent summer gardens for drinking and dining. Gardens in which performances were given seem to have become increasingly popular with the growth of family concert saloons, though they were not unknown before. Some later gardens obviously seated more spectators than did traditional concert saloons; probably this was partly a function of the fact that they had begun to cater to family audiences and needed more space than male-oriented saloons. No doubt, there was also the influence of German beer gardens, which tended to be large structures. In 1880, for example, the Atlantic Garden, a former German beer garden and hall – which now billed itself as "The Only Genuine Family Resort in America" and further boasted "Electric lights" – could hold over a thousand spectators, presumably both inside the hall and in its garden. (Gardens devoted to performance were fairly common later on top of theatres and other buildings, both in New York and elsewhere. They were employed as performance spaces or ballrooms, or sometimes as both.) Of course the famous Koster and Bial's cabaret, while not a garden as such, had a garden motif. At least one traditional concert saloon – probably more – seems to have had something that arguably was one. Asmodeus says, "By a long flight of stairs, we entered one of these concert-saloons, which, according to the sign, promised to be a spacious and shady garden. But . . . the walls alone represented the garden in highly inflamed patches of red, green, and yellow paint."

All in all, the typical New York concert saloon – at least the classic male-oriented one of the war years and after – seems to have been relatively small, similar to most other institutions of the same sort, and usually fairly limited in terms of decor. One imagines that most were not intended as theatres but were remodeled from their original function as saloons in order to house an audience, performers in some sort of show, recreational devices such as shooting galleries, and, in some cases, facilities for prostitution. Some concert saloons possessed proper stages and others apparently did not, having at best only a platform or simply a cleared space at ground level for what the Society called "performance." The majority seem not to have had balconies. Some had dancing by patrons, as well as shows.

In the final analysis, the spaces in many concert saloons were probably fairly crude and badly adapted to performance – they were often an afterthought designed to turn an ordinary saloon into a theatre of a sort. But drinking remained the chief business of the concert saloon. Shows – like waiter girls – were a novelty designed to bring in customers.

5

Employees and patrons of the concert saloon

Youngster, spare that girl!
Kiss not those lips so meek;
Unruffled let the fair locks curl
Upon the maiden's cheek!

Believe her quite a saint;
Her looks are all devine,
Her rosy hue is paint;
Her form is crinoline.

Poem on the waiter girl
in the *Clipper*, 1864

THE CONSENSUS AROUND NEW YORK WAS THAT THE CONCERT Bill spelled the death knell of the concert saloon. There was certainly a great deal of controversy, and of course many places did close. And some fired their waiter girls in order to comply with the law. As a matter of fact, the *Clipper* of November 26, 1864, maintained that the era of the "pretty waiter girl" was over and that all the concert saloons in New York had shut their doors. It was not so, of course, as the editors well knew. In the manner of such things, managers had established similar places in other cities, among them Baltimore and Washington. And a number of concert saloons would flourish in New York City, a number of them operating in basically the same way for some years to come.

The professional performers who appeared in concert saloons, both before and after the Concert Bill, were an anonymous lot, at or near the end of the social scale for all artists, who were themselves a largely rejected class. (In *Actors and American Culture*, Benjamin McArthur speaks of all itinerants as "at the bottom of the theatrical ladder.") For the most part, concert-saloon entertainers – basically itinerants – lived, performed their acts, and died, with little attention paid to them in the outside world, or even in the world of the theatre. The *Clipper*, and the Society documents, often did not even mention their names. In part for this reason, we know little about the lives or careers of most of the people who entertained in concert saloons. Those male entertainers who were mentioned by name by the Society for the Prevention of Juvenile Delinquency are listed in Appendix III. Women were another matter. Generally, their names were not mentioned.

Much the same thing was true for the musicians who specialized in concert-saloon work as for other performers. They were, by and large, not the artists who appeared in "respectable" middle-class concert halls like Steinway Hall, or even in the pit bands of legitimate theatres. They were chiefly untrained or half-trained performers who specialized in concert-saloon work and were ignored by more elevated artists. This did not keep some entertainers from putting on hightoned airs – even those at obvious dives. At one unnamed concert saloon, for example, Podhammer saw the "star of the evening," one "Signora" Johnson, sing "The Old Arm-Chair" with self-conscious flourishes, as follows:

> Hi lo-hove it, hi lo-hove it,
>   And who-oo sha-hall da-hare
> To-hoo chi-hi-hide me for lo-hoving
>   That o-ho-hold a-harm Cha-hair.

Most often, the exceptions to absolute obscurity were former stars – musicians or other popular performers – who tended to own, manage, or possess an interest in the saloons themselves or in small variety houses, or sometimes, like Robert Butler, to present an act as well. Butler, who had performed at several concert saloons and in pantomime and variety, became manager (and probably owner or part owner) of Butler's Varieties in 1860. He opened the Broadway Music Hall – often mentioned in this book – in the old Wallack's Theatre, 485 Broadway, once a legitimate house, in 1861.

If even legitimate theatres like Wallack's had a somewhat dubious reputation, concert saloons were associated in the public mind with every imaginable horror – and some only vaguely imaginable to middle-class people. Among them was homosexuality. There were almost certainly gay concert saloons (and a number of concert saloons that had gay patrons). But there is little extant information about any aspect of them, except the fact that homosexuals were considered a vice problem during the post-Civil War era. Generally, however, they were talked about – when they were talked about publicly – only in language that is not specific; the fear, however, was even more pronounced than the modern anxiety about gay bars and bath-houses and about their patrons as syphilitics or carriers of AIDS. The scanty evidence that remains suggests that at least a few of the gay saloons – for example, "Paresis Hall" at 392 Bowery – may have had shows, probably mostly presented by customers. But we know little about them. In an 1899 investigation, for example, we are told only that at Paresis Hall, "they had promised to give a show, as they call it, and it seems that the thing fell through." And in the same report, that the customers "get up and sing as women, and dance." There is, however, an interesting account in the New York *Times* of July 2, 1865, of a male concert-saloon worker who apparently was a transvestite and who was arrested in the Middle West. "Miss Addie," says the paper, is young, beautiful, and a flirt, and "posed as a woman," working as a waiter girl in concert saloons in New York for fourteen years, "remaining there until waiter girls were 'crushed,' when he went to Cleveland."

If no unauthorized mixing of the same sex was officially recognized in nineteenth-century New York, of course there was no unsanctioned mixing of the races. There certainly were ordinary saloons run for blacks. And so long as they had black patrons and staff, they seem to have been left more or less alone by the police. But little helpful detail is given in the newspapers and magazines of the day. The question of whether black saloons regularly presented shows of some kind is not known and is probably not discoverable. They seemingly did.

As Madelon Powers points out, fraternization was an ugly concept to many whites in the Northern as well as the Southern states. But even so there were the "black-and-tan" saloons of New York, where African Americans and whites met and mixed freely. (It was whispered that there were probably a large number of such places. Indeed, their rumored existence was felt by many nineteenth-century New Yorkers to suggest a serious social problem.)

And from time to time, of course, whites were found in black saloons of all kinds. But blacks were seldom seen in "white" concert or other saloons. It was too dangerous. At least one black performer, however, did appear in a predominantly white establishment, Carroll's. The star of the show for several years was a well-known black performer, Horace Westen. Westen, who lived from 1825 to 1890, had a remarkable talent for all things musical. He toured widely, in the United States, England, France, and Germany, with various minstrel companies, *Uncle Tom's Cabin* shows, and the circus.

Westen had long engagements at a number of New York City theatres and concert saloons, among them Carroll's, as well as at least one other concert-saloon in the eighties. His wife also played the banjo and often performed with him.

Following the Civil War, many African Americans also appeared in all-black minstrel troupes, often "blacking up" for shows, in imitation of white performers. Among them was Westen. Thus, there was nothing especially unusual about calling him, as the Society did, "a professional negro minstrel." But was it known that Westen was not simply a white performer wearing blackface? Did his audiences in concert saloons know that he was not white? Probably some did not – especially if he wore blackface makeup, as he may well have done.

But presumably many audience members *did* know. As "Champion Banjoist of the World," Westen had achieved a certain degree of notoriety. It is not hard to imagine, in fact, that many white spectators at a concert-saloon were aware that he was both famous and black. Perhaps they had seen him in another venue. Although a black performing with whites in a white institution was radical at the time, Westen did it, and the audience seemingly accepted it. Indeed, this kind of mixing of the races at the low end of New York's popular entertainment industry may well have been more common in the last quarter of the nineteenth century than is generally assumed. Podhammer wrote of a place on the Bowery at which the audience was "a diabolical-looking crowd of all shades of color, though the varieties of complexion were rendered scarcely distinguishable by a uniform coating of dirt – that leveler of distinctions."

This is not to make a case for excessive tolerance on the part of those whites who frequented such entertainment as the concert saloon. It may not have existed to any great degree. But a "live and let live" attitude may well have been present on the part of white concert-saloon audiences, at least toward acknowledged stars like Westen.

Thanks to random references in both the *Clipper* and in the Society papers, we know something about other kinds of concert-saloon workers. Many of the employees were probably Irish, a number of whom had come to the United States earlier in search of a better life. At the Boulevard, which styled itself a French resort, nobody spoke French, said the *Clipper*, and "the first two men and 'boy waiters' we met were natives of the land of the O'Donnells and Coburns." Some concert-saloon workers were said to be German and some were said to be Jews. We know, for example, that early concert saloons sometimes employed male waiters, in addition to the "pretty waiter girls," as well as kitchen and cleaning staff. (Male waiters seem to have been more common in the later years of the concert saloon, after the novelty of the "waiter girl" had largely worn off in New York.) There was vague speculation in papers and magazines that some boys who waited on customers were homosexual prostitutes.

At the Reveille in 1864, in addition to some twenty waiter girls, there were seven male waiters, two bartenders, and a cashier. There are many references to the bartenders in the *Clipper* articles, such as the man at the Champion Music Hall, who is described as personable and honest. He was "a sociable little fellow of light complexion, with light hair, whiskers and mustache . . . the last person to take advantage of or overcharge men somewhat the worse for 'small ales.'" But all were not so innocuous. At Billy Allen's Occidental there was William, who stood behind the bar in his shirt sleeves, "with a 'spark' in his bosom, dazzling as the dew drop . . . and another circling his sinister lilly-white fin." "Asmodeus," a French visitor in the post-Civil War era, wrote in his travel book, *Asmodeus in New York*, that "it is a business of no small importance to be a bar-tender – to thoroughly understand how to prepare the almost infinite number of beverages appreciated by the Americans."

Owners and managers are mentioned both in the *Clipper* articles and the Society documents. But for different reasons. The Society created rather cut-and-dried references designed to be used in court: "That, as deponent is informed and believes," read a typical form in 1875, "defendant A. O'Donnell was the manager and proprietor of such exhibition and that said defendant A. O'Donnell was the owner." Owners and managers are often mentioned ominously in Society documents as being present at – and sometimes emceeing – the shows held in concert saloons. "The owner of the building, place and premises was A. O'Donnell," said a Society document, "and that said defendant A. O'Donnell did advertise and set out to be, and allow himself to be the manager and proprietor of said 'O'Donnell's' or 'Gramercy Hall' and caused and aided in, allowed, consented to and abetted the exhibition of said performances."[1]

The *Clipper*, on the other hand, was interested in owners and managers (often the same person) because they tended to be colorful types. And perhaps because they possessed a great deal of influence in the lower reaches of the entertainment community, on which the *Clipper* depended. At one of the concert saloons, for example, its reporter commented: "Al Howard – a gay and festive young sport, a man amongst men, a jolly good fellow, and a good American – is the proprietor of the Boulevard."

Owen (or "Ownie") Madden was a kind of folk hero in concert saloons. Madden was an actual person, profiled in the 1920s by Herbert Asbury, the great historian of New York lowlife. In *The Gangs of New York*, Asbury paints a picture of a deceptively gentle sociopath. Madden, he says, "was slim, dapper, with the gentle smile of a cherub and the cunning and cruelty of a devil. He was born in England but came to the United States when he was eleven and was only seventeen when he got the name of Owney the Killer ... He was a crack shot with a revolver, an accomplished artist with the slung shot, a blackjack, and a pair of brass knuckles, not to mention a lead pipe wrapped in a newspaper, always a favorite weapon of the thug."[2]

After a long and checkered career as gang member, dive owner, and sometime murderer ... he started the Marginal Club, at 129 Eighth Avenue, above a saloon. "There he was shot though the heart a few months later [in 1919]," as Asbury has it, "by a man who approached him as he sat at a table with his back to the door." According to Asbury, Madden left an estate valued at about 100,000 dollars, then a considerable sum of money.

Women, of course, were very much present as concert-saloon workers. Several concert saloons had "cigar girls," the cigarette girls of a later day. At least one, the Bowery Music Hall, had a "lady cashier" in 1879. Although managements were largely male, a few women ran concert saloons. And just as many male owners came from the popular stage or the sporting or saloon worlds, a number of female owners seem once to have been associated with dance or the popular theatre. Generally, the women were particularly well liked by patrons. The *Clipper*, for example, wrote that Kate Stanton, a former jig dancer, who apparently owned the Champion Music Hall, was, "A lady of agreeable manners and conversation, and possesses a pair of the most fascinating eyes a woman could have. In her dancing days the boys used to swear by Kate Stanton. And whenever she appears for benefits, from the hearty reception which everywhere greets her, it is evident that she is as popular as ever on the mimic stage."[3] Stanton died in 1865.

It is a commonplace of most casual references to concert saloons, that they were always "all male"; that is, that no women other than waiter girls, prostitutes, and female entertainers ever set foot in most of them. Of course this is not true; women were clearly in the audience at many of the traditional concert saloons (not to mention "family" establishments), especially as time went on. Traditional concert saloons were by no means "respectable" venues, but they did provide cheap or free entertainment.

In a few places, however, women patrons were not let inside, especially during the Civil War period when concert saloons were largely male oriented. As the *Clipper* said of Lee and Hatstatt's Eureka, "A small card tacked to the door informs the public that 'No ladies are admitted,' wherefor or why not, as we are not in the business, we can't tell; but no such arbitrary rule has met our eye in other places." Increasingly, of course, after the Civil War, women were beginning to attend traditional concert saloons, often with escorts. But many saloons, according to reformers, always catered to a clientele that included "fast" women, who were not professional prostitutes but unescorted female customers looking for men. If concert saloons were not themselves houses of prostitution, then they were thought to be promoters of licentious behavior among the inmates, especially the women who went there unescorted. A number of Society documents of the 1870s, for example, make particular mention of females who sat at tables with men, smoking and drinking. A Society report devoted to the Newport in 1879 speaks of women of a "loose character" being present.

Some traditional concert saloons seem to have been used by male patrons for assignations, and the renting of rooms by the hour was not unknown. A number of females, Mc Cabe said, came from outside specifically for illicit trysts in rooms supplied by concert saloons. He picks one. "Observe the couple descending the steps," he says. He is a "handsome, most noble looking man," but with "his countenance stamped [with] the mark of a dissolute life." He is on the arm of a lover. He "whispers a word in the ear of one of the [waiter] girls, a meaningful smile flickers over her face as she hands him the key, with which he opens a door in the end of the room, and disappears with the female. Reader, you have seen a half dozen similar couples arrive and vanish through the same door. Do you know the why and wherefore of this proceeding? The saloon is one of the most *notorious assignation houses* in New York."[4]

Waiter girls, of course, were ubiquitous at concert saloons during the Civil War era. The *Evening Post* described them at the Novelty in rather unflattering terms in 1862: "There are about a dozen female waiters, mostly coarse-looking girls." They walked around "with a defiant swing and swagger" and drank, smoked cigars, and routinely chatted up and sat with male customers. Many concert saloons of the Civil War years, some in the seventies, and even a few in the eighties, of course, employed "pretty waiter girls." But the waiter-girl craze gradually disappeared after the Civil War, in part the victim of a changing morality.

According to Mc Cabe, the waiter girls of New York in his era were uniformly repulsive hags, and he makes no distinction between them and prostitutes. "The girls," he says, "are hideous and unattractive, and are foul-mouthed and bloated." Without exception, they are "prostitutes of the lowest order." This may or may not actually have been the case. But there is no doubt that waiter girls were non-persons and any contact with them was never to be mentioned in conversation with respectable people. The first names of waiter girls appear in documents from time to time, but their last names almost never. In all of the documents, the supposed full name of only one – a Jenny Clark, possibly a pseudonym – is mentioned. (As Odell says, a book with the names and faces of waiter girls was published in the nineteenth century – much like the guides to prostitutes of the era. But apparently it no longer exists.)

About a waiter girl and a customer, Mc Cabe says: "She is exerting all her arts to entice 'greeny into her net, and before long will be counting the amount of his cash; while he, her dupe, will, too late, be reflecting on the depravity of pretty waiter girls." As for their dangerousness, in his *New York By Gaslight*, he wrote, "They keep watch over their visitors, and when one of the latter, overcome with liquor, staggers out of the place, follow him, lure him into a back street, rob him, and, if necessary to their own safety, murder him. Oftentimes they lure their helpless victim to the river front, and there rob and kill him, and throw his body into the water, where it is found by the harbor police."

Mc Cabe presents a rather melodramatic picture of an innocent young woman who has been lured into becoming a waiter girl – and has been "ruined" along the way. She is, Mc Cabe says, "a fair sample (excuse the mercantile term) of her class":

> Not unprepossessing in appearance by any means Ellen – that, she tells us, is her name – is twenty-two years of age, was born in the village of Tarrytown, resided with her parents until she was eighteen, when her father died. Leaving her mother with her youngest brother, she came to New York seeking employment.

In the big city, of course, she meets with misfortune after misfortune. She was employed by a millinery store, but either left after a short time or was fired:

> [She] was out of work, had no friends, no money, would not go back to her mother who was poor, saw an advertisement of Madame —— for 'pretty waiter girls,' answered it, was engaged in the saloon, seduced (partly by promises and partly by threats), by one of the frequenters of the establishment and has since led the life of a prostitute.[5]

Ellen told her story to Mc Cabe "without the least emotion" and when asked about her mother carelessly replied that she imagined that she was dead by now.

The *Clipper* offered a very different view. Waiter girls were generally good looking – though of course there were exceptions – and they were essentially harmless. At Prescott Hall, for example, a reporter wrote that waiter girls "are only retained during good behavior; and the moment they begin to kick in the traces, away they go." At the Boulevard, a waiter girl named Emma was "ladylike, and all that. Her conversation was elegant and refined, and her demeanor fit for a White House drawing room." The *Clipper*, while reasonably realistic, was good natured about them. A reporter at the Champion Music Hall joked that he took a fancy to one of the girls who resembled a "deceased lady friend," and begged the printer not to substitute "diseased." Another reporter found the girls at the Saint Nicholas Casino reasonably representative. There were some plain ones, but "the majority are fine, buxom lasses," he said, "and the attendant at the cigar stand has one of the most magnetic and interesting faces we ever met. They treat all alike during good behavior, which is more than the authorities at Washington do."

Perhaps a somewhat more realistic view was provided by "Asmodeus":

> The whole force of female waiters was in attendance – that is, about thirty or forty young women, all busy endeavoring to quench the thirst of several hundred men; and while executing the "multitudinous orders" given them, they found sufficient time to distribute their photographs, to talk, and to drink with visitors. I noticed that they consumed nearly as much as the men, and wonder how they could stand it . . . The excesses of the poor creatures are sure to bring their miserable lives to an untimely end.[6]

Usually from or six or eight to perhaps forty waiter girls, from age fourteen to about thirty, were employed in New York concert saloons. A number of them seem to have come from minor jobs in dance or the theatre. Indeed, the stage was widely believed – perhaps not altogether incorrectly – to be a training ground for them. A reporter for the *Clipper* wrote about the waiter girls at the Oriental that "many of them have been at one time or another ballet girls, or in some other occupation on the stage in this city."

About the waiter girls at the Reveille, the *Clipper* commented that they received a "fair remuneration" of five dollars a week for four hours a night, six evenings a week, "and its no wonder that many leave home to tend in concert halls so as to keep from actual starvation." But the waiter girls obeyed strict rules. These rules were set down in the *Clipper* article, and demonstrated a tendency for management to adopt a take-it-or- leave-it policy with their often hungry workers:

> You will please take notice that on and after this date no checks will be given to any girl coming to the saloon at fifteen minutes before eight o'clock. And you will also take notice that on pay nights no girl will get her money [if she?] does not get to the saloon on that night.

> Also take notice that no girl will be allowed to stay at home on Saturday nights, unless in case of sickness, as by doing so she will forfeit her situation, and under no circumstances whatever will any girl be allowed to stay home over one night in each week, without forfeiting two nights' salary for each night. Also, from this date the doors will be locked at a quarter before eight o'clock and will not be opened to admit any girl. And the above rules and regulations will be strictly carried out.[7]

In many respects, the mid-nineteenth-century waiter girl was the ancestor of the more modern "B-girl." The chosen patrons were expected to pay for the girl's drinks – usually at inflated prices – as well as their own. Even the *Clipper* admitted as much, pointing out that the object of time spent in a concert saloon was to get rid of as much money as possible. The "checks" mentioned in the rules at the Reveille were cashed by the management. Some concert saloons employed tokens instead. Asmodeus explains the system. Concert-saloon owners, he says, paid their waiter girls too little to live on. In order to increase it, "they purchase every morning a certain number of drinking-tickets . . . at a discount of thirty percent and sometimes more. If you follow their motions, you will perceive that they themselves keep the money received from visitors, and pay the bartender with their own tickets, on obtaining from him the ordered refreshments." In order to get rid of the largest number of tickets, Asmodeus continues, "the girls have recourse to all conceivable stratagems – the most usual being to ask the visitor to drink a toast to their beauty. Though the latter is generally faded; and as the Hebe has to keep him company while toasting her charms, he pays for two drinks instead of one."[8] In any case, "the more custom [the waiter girls] get at the bar, the better it is for them individually." At the New Oriental, for example, they received an unnamed bonus for every fancy drink sold, and for every bottle of wine, fifty cents.

In later years an old police detective, John Warren, presented a rather jaundiced view of the charms of many waiter girls that helps put the *Clipper*'s accounts into perspective. He says in his book *Thirty Year's Battle With Crime*: "The waist of these fleshy beauties is the only part of them that boasts a covering of any sort." He found them "huge limbed and squabby." They illustrate, he said, "the low breed of human animal from which they spring," and "on closer inspection, their manners, habits, language, and tastes will be found in perfect harmony with their exterior habits."

Without doubt waiter girls recognized that they were in a male-oriented tourist business of a sort; they were, in fact, among the popular sights – and sounds – of the city during and after the Civil War. They may not automatically have been prostitutes, but they were certainly expected to serve as many patrons as possible, and probably to promise much, even if they failed to deliver. One also hears a great deal of their facility at conversing with men. They were geishas of a sort, chatting up males as part of their always insecure jobs. "Every masculine group had their feminine friend," said the *Clipper*, about one place, "and out of the twenty-five ladies of the place, it would puzzle a Baptist deacon to tell who attracted the most notice." At the Reveille, it was worth the trip, said the *Clipper*, "to stop in some night – or rather some morning, for business don't commence till 'dog watch' on shipboard – to study the manners and habits of these morning glories and hear their critiques. Talk about mocking birds and parrots being noisy, there din isn't a circumstance to the chatter-chatter of these waiting maids. Every little thing that has transpired in their respective saloons is peddled out in regular gossipy style, for here their tongues have full sway." The proprietors "care not while exchanging their provender for dirty bits of paper representing money" and "nobody attempts to stay the raging billows of woman's tongue. We stayed in there one night and the noise of their chatter boxes seems to buzz in our ears yet."⁹

There is no denying that some were good at it. And the gambits were not all conversational. At another concert saloon, the *Clipper* reporter discovered Fanny, a friend of a former sweetheart of his, which "made us friends right off." She was, he wrote, probably the best known waiter girl in New York, with a style "better adapted to make the fellows stay longer than any other girl." This was in part due to "the liberality with which she exhibits her figure . . . dropping her cambric and stooping down to pick it up so as to let the young fellows see there's nothing artificial, and so forth." He ends by saying that all the young bucks "speak well of Fanny."

As acknowledged curiosities for male tourists, waiter girls were often expected to dress in a distinctive way. Most wore ordinary dresses, but a costume consisting of a short skirt and high red boots, often with bells or tassels, was favored by some. The "theme" establishments, a *Clipper* reporter thought, featured costumes that were provided by management. At the Oriental, for example, they appeared in the "national color of old Ireland – bright green; in Turkish costume, with turbans and trouserloons gathered in tight around the ankle; in the Highland plaids, with a rare opportunity to display their symmetrical limbs; and, in fact, in the dress of all nations but the Patagonians, who wear little or nothing, you know."[10]

At the so-called New Oriental, "one of the girls had on the Polynesian costume, a second the Japonican, another the Sclavonian." Of some thirty handsome "girls in attendance, no two are rigged alike, all being dressed in the national and picturesque costumes of Europe." One was "attired a la Child of the Regiment, with short crimson skirt, black velvet jippo, braided across her heaving bosom with gold lace bands, after the approved military fashion."

We know that waiter girls sometimes also worked as entertainers during the Civil War era, often singing songs or playing musical instruments for patrons. At many concert saloons of the day, for example, waiter girls seem not only to have brought drinks to customers, but to have been expected to appear onstage, if they played a musical instrument or could carry a reasonable tune. Perhaps it was a requirement for the job, and certainly many of the waiter girls also were sometime performers. In any event, as the *Clipper* pointed out, in 1864, at the Boulevard, "on the road to [McComb's] dam," "a couple of the 'sprites,' as alike as two peas, sang a very sweet duet together, accompanied by [the versatile] Walter Smith on the violin and Piano Tom on the piano. Their names we cannot recall, but many who are cracked up as Irish Nightingales, English Thrushes, Black Swans, etc., are not a marker to these same lady amateurs. After the duet, one of them sang that pretty ballad, written by Charles McKay and set to music by H. Russell, entitled 'Sunshine After Rain,' the sentiments of which are exceedingly beautiful."[11]

The Victorians were no strangers to pornography, and from time to time, however, it was a racy song. A waiter girl sang a mildy salacious song at the Opera Saloon in 1864 which told the story of a man who was falsely alleged to be the father of a baby conceived by an ugly woman. It ended:

> Three dollars a week I had to pay
> To Nancy, Miss Nancy,
> I never was there I do declare
> And that's what I don't fancy.

Or perhaps there was the one quoted in Richard O'Conner's *Hell's Kitchen* as often being sung at Sunday "sacred concerts," mandated for all kinds of public places by the city's Blue Laws and rather casually adhered to by theatres and concert saloons:

> Georgie, Georgie, pray give over,
> Georgie, Georgie, you're too free.
> Stop your palaver, else I'll tell Father,
> Georgie, give over and let me be.

Or perhaps patrons heard the song mentioned by Douglas Gilbert in *American Vaudeville*, which contained this chorus:

> So sit down by my side and don't feel alarm
> At my Hi dinky doodle dum day.

But, by and large, the songs sung in most concert saloons appear to have been innocuous or only mildly suggestive at worst.

Waiter girls frequently challenged (or were challenged by) male patrons at the shooting galleries found in so many concert saloons. (The shooting galleries may have been rigged; in any case, usually the waiter girls won, much to the chagrin of the defeated men.) As the *Clipper* had it, during the Civil War, at Shafer's Eureka:

> A fast youth of twenty five, more or less, either a counter or a bounty jumper, was trying his abilities with one of the coryphees – a bright-eyed, innocent looking girl – as to who should pay the fiddler as well for a bottle of vintage. But he hadn't the ghost of a chance.... The bell rang and...a young virgin sprang from the left side or wherever the deuce they come from. For six times in succession, Miss Nancy turned the man into a woman by hitting the target in the small black circle, while the young swell couldn't begin to do so, at least not in that basement.[12]

At the Opera Saloon a girl nick-named Eugene challenged the reporter for the *Clipper*. He "respectfully declined." But the waiter girl was having none of it. "With commendable perseverance, Eugene froze fast and declared she could just knock us sky high when it came to shooting. 'Guess not, daughter.' 'I guess yes, sonny.'" The reporter soon changed his mind; he was soundly beaten, whereupon the waiter girl casually went off to sing a song.

During the Civil War, then, the job of waiter girl was filled by poor, badly educated women who had little choice in the matter; jobs in concert saloons were among the few open to women, especially those with little or no education or training. They may not have been prostitutes – and some were undoubtedly part-time entertainers. Still in all, "concert saloon" had become a synonym for house of prostitution and generally no so-called respectable woman wanted to work in one, or even to set foot in one.

And then there were the out-and-out prostitutes. Information about concert-saloon prostitutes is scanty and vague, and the extent to which concert saloons regularly employed prostitutes is not known; certainly, reformers thought they did. There is little doubt, in any case, that some concert saloons were clearly fronts for prostitution. In *Their Sister's Keepers: Prostitution in New York City, 1830–1870*, Marilyn Wood Hill writes that "the concert-saloon rose in popularity at the same time the New York theatre was restricting prostitutes in its effort to become more respectable, thus filling a 'leisure-entertainment recruiting' void for some women in the prostitution business as well as a general cultural void for New Yorkers who wanted cheap but lively entertainment."[13] A *Clipper* reporter wryly noted that a certain very prominently displayed picture at the What Is It was of a voluptuous nineteenth-century dancer who, as it said, "first danced upon one leg and then the other, and between the two she made her living . . ."

Alvin Harlow, in his classic study of the heart of the cheap entertainment district, *Old Bowery Days and Ways*, quotes one of the concert-saloon owners as saying, "A concert-saloon is a ginmill on an improved plan, that's all, my friend." At one level this is quite true. In any case, a traditional concert-saloon in any period was not merely another place to drink, but a saloon that featured a show of some kind, alleged to be racy, as well as supposedly "loose" women.

There is no reason to think that a traditional concert-saloon resembled the ubiquitous working man's saloon, with its loyal crowd of "regulars," to which Madelon Powers devotes most of *Faces along the Bar*. The concert saloon, in fact, was quite different from the saloon on the corner. As was mentioned earlier, *Valentine's Manual* linked it with twentieth-century night clubs, the low end of which it resembled in many ways. Certainly, it can also be traced to the beginnings of burlesque and other entertainments that essentially depended on sexual display. As Mc Cabe points out, with some apparent accuracy, although with a certain melodramatic quality, the usual concert-saloon featured a raffish, but otherwise diverse crowd. "At a table nearly opposite our own," he says, "are seated a couple, one of whom at least, to even the casual observer, is a stranger to the place and surroundings. There is no doubt of it. Wholly enraptured by the beauty and grace of his female companion [a waiter girl], he is totally oblivious to all passing around." By this time, says Mc Cabe, a typical saloon is crowded with

> men and women of all degree of social standing. Here is the man-about-town, the hanger-round of hotels, in clothes of unquestionable cut and make, talking earnestly with a female whose drawn veil conceals her face – perhaps some unfortunate victim of his lust, or probably his mistress, come to plead for justice, or her week's allowance of money. Yonder is a youth of . . . "some eighteen summers," young in years but old in sin, who supports on his knee a *nymph du pave*, with whom he has entered from the street, and upon whom he is spending his last quarter's salary, or the proceeds of an investigation into the till of his employer.[14]

But there were other factors at work. The Civil War, like any war, had created moral conservatism, especially among politicians, at the same time that it spurred an increasing need for all kinds of entertainment to take the minds of the public off its troubles. In this case, it led to the push by prominent managers to get rid of the competition and to sweep under the rug any connection between prostitution and the theatre. These fears were almost certainly partly responsible for the Concert Bill passing with few problems.

Conservative commentors (including representatives of the Society) were also very much concerned that, during the war years, concert saloons were the haunts of military men on leave (which was bad for the already tarnished reputation of New York City). In a sense, all the conservative commentors were quite correct – military men *did* frequent concert saloons.

One reads in contemporary accounts that officers and enlisted men from the army came in large numbers to concert saloons, especially during the Civil War; for some reason, sailors seem to have been more attracted to dance houses. In one article, the writer said, for example, that, "its no use talking, the concert-saloon business is mainly supported by soldiers, as the Fourth Ward dance houses are by sailors." In a burst of candor, the *Clipper* wrote that, at the Bon Ton, "there were army and navy officers, who should have been with [*sic*] the bosom of their family." In a corner of an unnamed concert saloon, Mc Cabe spied a soldier, just returned from the Civil War, who had recently been paid off, and who is now "expending his hard-earned pittance of the government upon some bepainted and bedizened courtesan, while perhaps his wife and family are suffering for want of the common necessities of life." About the Champion Music Hall, for instance, the *Clipper* pointed out that "it is fairly astonishing to see the numerous military men who resort to these saloons for recreation, and to while away a hour or two in company with affable and interesting females."

In a "room full of soldiers," the *Clipper* reporter said, a waiter girl sang a song that ended in tribute to soldiers. A mere fighter, she sang, will never win a woman; but a soldier was another matter. The song ended:

> But a soldier boy whose blows
> Fall on his country's foes,
> When the ring is pitched, the battle-field will win.

As military men knew, the atmosphere in many concert saloons could be a little rough – which probably only added to the attractiveness of such places. At any rate, both sides did admit that fights often took place. Mc Cabe described the situation in a somewhat Dickensian way in *Secrets of the Great City*. "A cry of pain, followed by a burst of brutal laughter," he said, reconstructing an evening's events in one concert saloon, "causes us to turn our eyes to the corner just in time to witness a woman fall to the ground, felled by a blow from the clenched fist of the brute with whom she had been quarreling. For a moment there is silence in the hall, but only for a moment. The girl is picked up by her companions – a few rough jokes at her expense – and all goes on as before. Such scenes are of too frequent occurrence to provoke comment."[15]

The *Clipper*, on the other hand, was scarcely concerned about the damage to persons or property, except for the injustice being done to concert-saloon proprietors and their staffs by the Concert Bill. The *Clipper* had no trouble admitting that there was often raucous behavior in concert saloons, and did so on several occasions. In its article about Ballard's What Is It, for example, the paper noted that "scarcely a night in the year rolled around but *lex talonis* is the motto between man and man, and that somebody doesn't get mauled. It's a pretty warm neighborhood, 'vich nobody will deny.'" But the paper maintained that everything was generally under control. At the Reveille, the owner, E. A. Simpson "employs two deputy sheriffs to attend to these matters," it said, "and there is never any chance for a disturbance. And he feels proud to have it said that in four long years there has never been an *emeute* in the *estaminet*."

Of course, the reason for the Society's support of the Concert Bill probably lay to some degree in the fact that concert saloons actively contributed to what the middle classes felt was the delinquency of the city's youth. After all, prevention of delinquency was their mission. The reformers and quasireformers also had their say. Mc Cabe says, in regard to young people, for instance: "Turn into any of the concert or dance halls, and you will find the majority of those present to be young men and girls not out of their teens." In a way, concert saloons *did* contribute to juvenile delinquency. It is certainly true, in any case, that young people flocked to them. Commentors of the day make a point of mentioning them as constantly in attendance, and of course the Society for the Prevention of Juvenile Delinquency was much concerned.

But all kinds of patrons frequented the concert saloons. As the *Evening Post* said about the Novelty: "Owing to the moderate price, the place is generally crowded, especially on a Saturday night..." Of course, criminals and toughs were among the crowd. There is no doubt, however, that most establishments were the haunts of men who were perhaps somewhat fast but basically respectable. They were often – in the vernacular of a later day – simply "slumming." Some patronized concert saloons of the higher sort, which catered to them, the Boulevard may have been one of them. The *Clipper*, at any rate, saw a number of such men – there were "no cropped heads or red shirts, or high brimmed hats, or tight corduroys," the marks of the tough. Instead, one encountered "respectable, well dressed businessmen, met together for social and rational enjoyment."

Indeed, in its article on the Champion Music Hall, the *Clipper* said that "the 'bloods'... keep most of our underground palaces going, but every other class in the community is represented in these same places, even to the sleek-faced parson or pussey elder from Tomatosville." In the Bon Ton, for example, every sort except "lushingtons and boys" was present in the main room behind the screen. But at the reporter's table were distinctly middle-class types, including an alderman, an auctioneer, a tobacconist, and a physician. At the New Oriental, says the *Clipper*, "by the veritable toe-nail of Methuselah, if there wasn't two of our most famous city judges shooting a match [in a shooting galley], we hope to die."

Many of the frequenters of concert saloons in any time, however, were working-class men, out for a night on the town. They were not precisely toughs, and not exactly professional men or prosperous merchants, but rather ordinary mechanics and small tradesmen on a spree. The *Clipper*, for example, mentions a "fire laddie" in the ubiquitous red shirt worn by volunteer firemen and a goatee, "like Ogden, the Irish ambassador."

Perhaps the classic visitors to concert saloons, though, were the "gentlemen from the country" – by which the *Clipper* really meant "rubes" or "hayseeds." They were "mentioned with tongue in cheek at the Opera Saloon." The country types were "going it very lively," said the *Clipper*,

about a group that had read about concert saloons in the New York papers.
They had made a special visit "on the strength of reading about the saloons,
to see for themselves the *modus operandi*."

Everyone was incensed by the – very frequent – presence of boys and
old men among the patrons. Even the *Clipper* objected to the "staid old
fogies who ought to have been through the mill thirty years ago, sitting
face to face with young damsels, comely to look upon and very agreeable
company." And at Lee and Hatstatt's Eureka, the reporter surmised that the
watch beside the bar, which was to be raffled off, probably was "the property
of some old sport who lives too fast for his income." At the Bon Ton it noted
reassuringly that neither boys nor drunken soldiers were allowed behind the
screen where the shows took place and the waiter girls were to be found:
"The screen is put there for the express purpose of keeping out the young
aristocratic snips with more money than brains, who ape the man and are
made to sweat for it. If instead of finding fault with the girls for making these
snobs pay for the whistle, if the papers and authorities were to advocate a
little birch rod on their nether end, it would be far more effectual and just."[16]

One thing was true beyond a doubt: that there was (almost certainly
illegal) gambling taking place in many concert saloons. In fact, one would be
surprised if it was not present. It probably added to their appeal. The *Clipper*
phrased it this way with regard to the patrons at Lee and Hatstatt's Eureka:
sometime after midnight, the reporter found, "the halls of Pharaoh were just
then beginning their little game; and while the gamboliers [*sic*] were sowing
or reaping, the strangers and representatives of the army and navy, with what
was left of their greenbacks, were thinking of turning in for the night."[17]

In short, the concert-saloon existed, not for regulars, but for every sort
of "fast" men, "respectable" men, boys and girls, for soldiers and sailors, for
working men out for a night on the town, and for visitors from the country
and from other towns and cities, who had heard how things were carried out
in New York. And it genuinely transcended the usual class, gender – and
perhaps to some extent – racial lines. As the *Clipper* had it in its article on
Frank Burns' Oriental: "It's no rare thing to see lawyer and client, judge and
juryman, master and servant, hobnobbing together over their Stoughton
Bitters or Root Beer with a buxom lass beside them, talking politics or
whatnot, so as to enable visitors to spend a pleasant time and induce them
to call again."[18]

A clear split governed the views of the traditional concert saloons and its
inmates: some people felt that concert saloons were either more or less

harmless establishments; others felt that they were in fact dives, each one fouler than the next. Some felt that all females connected with concert saloons were part-time prostitutes; others that they were simply attractive working-class women who were making the only kind of living they could. That is, one's view largely depended on which side one was on, the reformers' or the concert saloon proponents'. In fact – in the early years, at least – anyone who worked in concert saloons, especially the already-suspect performers, were overwhelmingly considered little better than the waiter girls, who themselves were widely considered to be little better than prostitutes. Male patrons of all sorts, on the other hand, seemed to be able to go to the traditional concert saloons with a certain impunity. All in all, that was the beginning and the end of it for most middle-class people.

6

Related forms

Nearly half the company consisted of women and children.

New York *Times*, on a German beer garden, December 27, 1858

From five to a dozen women, so bloated and horrible to look at, that a decent man shudders with disgust as he beholds them, are lounging about the room. They have reached the last step in the downward career of fallen women, and will never leave this place until they are carried to their graves, which are not far distant.

James Mc Cabe, Jr., on the inmates of dance houses, *Lights and Shadows of New York Life*, 1872

TWO NINETEENTH-CENTURY POPULAR-ENTERTAINMENT FORMS that were related to the New York City concert saloon were the dance house and the German beer garden. Though both the dance house and the beer garden were quite different from each other and from the concert saloon, both influenced it in certain ways and both were influenced *by* it. In addition, the dance house and the German beer garden both symbolized a division that was beginning to exist within the concert saloon itself after the war. The dance house and the people associated with it were suspect – it was male-oriented, primarily involved with sexuality, or at least the promise of sex. The German beer garden was a different matter. It was aggressively family-oriented and attempted to be scrupulously uncontroversial. In later years, however, the German beer gardens were investigated – for whatever reasons – by the Society. As an earlier chapter explains, there may have been a financial motive.

The German beer gardens (most of them selling no hard liquor, only beer, wine, and soft drinks), were aimed at the nineteenth-century German families who lived and worked on the Lower East Side of New York. They

should not be confused with the German establishments that catered principally to men – although there were, of course, German concert saloons,
gambling houses, houses of prostitution, and the like.

The Germans had begun to arrive in New York City as early as the
seventeenth century, though it was not until the nineteenth century that
they came in great numbers and began to have a considerable impact on
the city's cultural life. By 1840, almost 25,000 Germans and Austrians lived
there. By 1880 there were 370,000 in New York City, about a third of the total
population. German immigration reached a peak in 1900. There were almost
800,000 Germans, partly as a result of the January 1, 1898, consolidation,
which annexed to Manhattan, Brooklyn, The Bronx, Queens, and Staten
Island, in order to form the greater City of New York. Immigration to New
York City from German-speaking countries trailed off in the twentieth
century.

Until the turn of the century, a third of all the immigrants were concen-
trated in "Kleindeutchland," an area in Manhattan made up of the Bowery
and adjacent parts of the Lower East Side. Others settled in Williamsburg
in Brooklyn, and Hoboken in New Jersey, and, by the 1870s, in Yorkville
in Manhattan and in various parts of Queens. The main street of Kleindeutchland was the old Bowery Road itself, also known in the nineteenth-
and early-twentieth centuries as New York's cheap entertainment area. The
Bowery had been the access road to Peter Stuyvesant's farm in the seventeenth century. It remained on the fringes of New York until about 1800, but
was important as the main road to Boston. Starting in the early nineteenth
century, it became, first, a major residential street and, later, the site of all
sorts of entertainment. The Bowery was lined with minstrel houses, oyster
bars, and taverns. It was also the home of the famous Bowery Theatre, built
in 1826, which began as a first-class house, and by mid-century had begun
specializing in melodrama and spectacle and other popular favorites.

Germans had begun to move into the area around the Bowery in part because of the low rents in the area and in part because other German-speakers
had already settled there. *Harper's New Monthly Magazine* wrote in 1871
that the street had become – as well as a "low" entertainment center – the
nucleus of a German "city within a city." The magazine had to admit, however, that, as the center of Kleindeutchland, "the Bowery has a respectability
of its own."

But after the Civil War the street increasingly had become known for its
saloons, cheap shops, and such low-cost amusements as dime museums –
and of course the concert saloons. By the end of the nineteenth century,

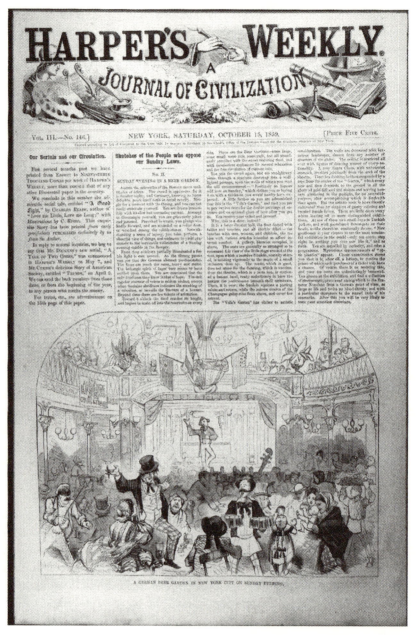

9 "A German Beer Garden in New York City on Sunday Evening," *Harper's Weekly*,
October 15, 1859

when Yorkville was becoming the center of German culture, the Bowery was becoming a skid row, infamous as the center of alcoholism and wretchedness. But throughout much of the nineteenth century, the Bowery was an entertainment center *and* the New York home of the German immigrant.

Among them, ties were strong to Germany and the German language. One result was a profusion of German beer gardens on or near the Bowery. A few were aimed at Germans from particular regions, but most were simply for German speakers in search of harmless – even resolutely decorous – amusement in their free hours, like the kind of entertainment found everywhere in the fatherland. Some beer halls operated year round, with a "summer garden" in which beer and entertainment were available; others were principally "winter gardens," vast indoor halls also offering beer and mild amusements, usually innocuous and often centered around music – either popular or what we would call today "light classical." A number of beer gardens were elaborately decorated. Many were quite large.

Basically, the German beer gardens were inoffensive resorts, except to the most abstemious – or reform-minded – New Yorkers. Even Mc Cabe was forced to admit this fact. "The larger German music halls," he wrote, "have the only respectable audiences to be found in the city. To these the children of the Fatherland resort in great numbers to enjoy their beer and listen to the music. The husband and father takes his wife and family along with him, and the pleasure here is innocent and orderly."[1]

There were only a few public critics of the German beer garden. And most of the criticism consisted of somewhat half-hearted attacks on Sabbath-breaking, drinking, and the rather mild gambling games that characteristically took place there. There were far worse things to complain about than offenses like mild gambling. One of the gambling games – similar to Skittles – was called Tivoli; in addition to the usual billiards and a bar, said the *Times* in April of 1860, there was, at the Volksgarten, "an innocent little game in which you send a ball spinning among a lot of pins which, if touched by the ball, is placed to the credit of the player. You are admitted to the game on the payment of five cents; any number can play that choose; and the winner – the individual that makes the greatest count – takes two thirds of the money, the balance going to the Tivoli machine."

Another gambling game had been profiled in the *Times* in December of 1858. It featured a "small brass cannon from which balls are projected, probably by a spring. They descend by an inclined plane on which stand wooden pins. Ten tickets are given out, say at three cents each. The holder representing the greatest number of pins wins twenty cents, the balance of

10 Celebrating the Capitulation of the Sedan at the "Atlantic Garden," n.d.

the stakes – one third of the whole – going into the pocket of the proprietor."
At the Volksgarten, said the *Times*, there was also a gambling game with
dice, with prizes given for rolling an eight or forty-eight. In another game,
a patron sat on a wooden horse, holding a lance. "While the horse is made
to go round in a circle, he or she tries to spear an iron ring."

The *Times* mildly scolded those who found the ambiance of the beer
hall stimulating. It observed that Sunday attendance by young people was
not good for the moral health of the city, because "it brings a number of
young gentlemen there who would be much better employed in hearing
even a sensational minister preach." Perhaps because of its rather innocuous
gambling, the beer garden was seen by the more respectable as a dubious
influence on children. For example, the right-thinking *Times* pointed out in
1858, that, "Good men do not grow out of boys who spend their Sundays at
Volks Gartens and Volks Theatres." But supposed moral issues stopped few
Germans. The beer gardens were relatively cheap, familiar, and welcoming
places. Whole families gathered at a beer garden at the weekend to hear
music and see sketches from their homeland, presented in German and later
in English or another popular language like Yiddish: said the *Times* about
a beer garden in 1858, "a shilling admits you to the place, but you can take
your wife and children with you 'free.'" There is little evidence that anyone
resolutely thought most German beer gardens were really unwholesome, or
that most of their patrons were corrupted by them.

There were dozens of beer gardens around New York. Logically enough,
many of them were on or around the Bowery. In *Little Germany*, Stanley
Nadel says: "There were a number of the magnificent establishments (like
the Deutsches Volksgarten, the Atlantic Gardens, Nieblo's Saloon, Magar's
Concert Hall, and Lindenmeyer's Odeon) that provided Kleindeutschland
with centers of popular culture." A few were elegant and fantastic in the
manner of later movie palaces, many were simply large and comfortably appointed. About the Volksgarten, at 45 Bowery, for example, *Harper's Weekly*
said, it was "a large circular hall," the floor dotted with tables and benches,
and "all thickly filled." There were men, women, and children on the benches
and at the tables. "The tables [also contained] various articles intended to
afford internal comfort. A gallery, likewise occupied, is above. The seats are
generally so arranged as to command a fair view of the little stage erected
at the rear . . ."

The Atlantic Garden, 50 Bowery, occupied the site of an old stove fac-
tory and coal yard. Legend had it that part of the beer garden had been the
old Bull's Head Tavern, which Washington occupied as his headquarters

during the Revolution. Of it Mc Cabe said in *Lights and Shadows*, it was "the true beer garden." The Atlantic Garden was next door to the old Bowery Theatre; it was very large and high-ceilinged, and lit by a number of chandeliers and by sconces on its walls. About it, the *Century* said in 1891, "There is little about them [the Germans in New York] that is peculiar to us, but they maintain one notable resort, which is known and almost familiar wherever German is spoken." The Atlantic Garden, the *Century* said, "is the largest of the beer saloons. It is not only the resort of the Bowery Germans, but it is the rendezvous for the officers and crews of all the German vessels that come to the port and for a great many German tourists and travelers who are passing through the country" – and increasingly, after the turn of the nineteenth century, as German immigration declined, of the second generation, and of non-German-speaking families. Nonetheless, wrote the *Century*, the Atlantic was still "thoroughly German, from the dishes served on the counter near the door, to the music played by the orchestra within, or the well-salted pretzels that are consumed with the beer."[2]

In 1872 Mc Cabe described the interior of the main room in detail in *Lights and Shadows*:

> It is an immense room, with a lofty curved ceiling handsomely frescoed, and lighted by numerous chandeliers and by brackets along the walls. It is lighted during the day from the roof. At one side there is an open space planted with trees and flowers, the only part of a garden visible. A large gallery rises above the floor at each end. That at the eastern or upper end is used as a restaurant for those who desire regular meals. The lower gallery is like the rest of the place, for beer drinkers only. Under the latter gallery is a shooting hall, which is usually filled with marksmen trying their skills. On the right hand side of the room is a huge orchestrion or monster music box, and by its side is a raised platform, occupied by the orchestra employed at the place. The floor is sanded and lined with plain tables, six feet by two in size, to each of which is a couple of benches. The only ornaments of the immense hall are the frescoes and chandeliers. Everything else is plain and substantial.[3]

The *Century* described it some thirty years later. "It is simply a large hall," said the magazine, "a block in depth, partly surrounded by a gallery, and set with chairs and tables. Its decorations are neither good, bad, nor costly. All in all, in terms of physical appearance, it was not so very different from big dance houses or such elegant concert saloons as the Canterbury."[4] There was, however, a major difference. "It's purpose is to afford a place in which an hour can be passed in talking, drinking beer, and listening to a band by night and of a huge orchestrion by day." A fiftieth anniversary souvenir book from 1908 attached it to the Revolutionary past by stating as fact the often-repeated rumor that the main building had once been part of General Washington's famous Bull's Head Tavern.

The Atlantic Garden was resolutely a family place and no hint of impropriety was allowed. The decorousness was not merely skin-deep, as was the case of some places, but was a given; in fact, all of the German beer gardens seem to have been proper environments for respectable working men, their wives and their children. Mc Cabe studies the patrons in detail and creates a quaint little scene:

> The buzz and hum of the conversation, and the laughter are overpowering, and you wander through the vast crowd with your ears deafened by the sound. Suddenly, the leader of the orchestra raps sharply on his desk, and there is a prolonged silence over all the hall. On an instant the orchestra breaks forth in some wonderful German melody, or some deep voiced, strong lunged singer sends his notes rolling through the hall. The auditors have suddenly lost their merriment, and are now listening pensively to the music, which is good. They sip their beers absently and are thinking no doubt of the far off Fatherland, for see their features soften and their eyes glisten. Then when it is all over, they burst into encore, or resume their suspended conversations.[5]

"Disorder is almost unknown," admits the *Century*, in the same vein. "Women and children accompany husbands and fathers, and the drinking is performed with a dispassionate, thoroughly European regard for temperance and economy... A glass of beer is made to last a very long time there, and consequently to yield as much refreshment as half a dozen glasses taken as New Yorkers are apt to drink it." The entertainment at the Atlantic Garden, said the *Century*, was likewise, thoroughly unobjectionable. "The band is usually composed of a dozen well-trained women, dressed neatly, all alike, and as women would appear at a high-class musical entertainment. Breaking the music of this band a balladist or serio-comic singer appears at intervals during the evening."[6] As a matter of fact, the Atlantic Garden seems to have specialized in rigidly proper female entertainers. In his valuable *Old Bowery Days and Ways*, Alvin Harlow says that the "ladies orchestra" so popular in the German community began here – "not a man in it save the cornetist, and it was whispered that he was married to the trombone and they couldn't get rid of him."

German winter and summer gardens or beer gardens appear in many legal documents, articles, and illustrations of the period. These make quite clear that the bulk of the German beer gardens on or near the Bowery featured nothing suggestive, only dancers, comedians, opera singers, and other entertainers of interest to a German-speaking clientele, in addition to bands, popular singers, and mechanical music. (Late in the century they were attracting German, German-American, and native customers, and the presentations were no longer exclusively in German. The programs were more likely to include some English – or at least some Yiddish, since Jews were appearing frequently in the neighborhood.)

The beer gardens probably were direct ancestors of the late nineteenth- and early twentieth-century family-oriented saloons in the city, as well as the "gardens" that came to exist on top of theatres and other buildings. Certainly, their patronage began to shift to English speakers. In the early years of the twentieth century, beer gardens seem to have had the choice of either going out of business or welcoming new non-German-speaking customers. The Atlantic Garden, for example, could not compete with newer forms. It closed, and was torn down in 1916.

The successes or failure of German beer gardens, as well as their move- ment toward a broader, non-ethnic family patronage, seem always to have been watched by some concert-saloon owners and managers, who imitated it, creating family establishments of their own.

But there was a second model – the dance house, famous for both a popular early variety of taxi-dancing and as a front for prostitution. Many were owned by men, a few by women. The dance houses were thought to be heavily patronized by sailors on shore leave, just as it was thought that soldiers were major customers at the concert saloons. There was probably some truth to both beliefs, at least during the Civil War, although the military were far from the only customers of both institutions; many civilians were also patrons, both during and after the war. In any case, like concert saloons, dance houses generally featured music and, of course, dancing. They had bad reputations, especially with clergymen and other reformers, and with conservative people generally. Mc Cabe found dance houses even more sordid than concert saloons. "The dance houses," he wrote, "differ from the concert saloons in this respect, that they are one grade lower both as regards the inmates and the visitors, and that dancing as well as drinking is carried on in them."

But most dance houses did not feature acts at all, only social dancing and – if the many contemporary sources are be believed – prostitution. The rumors of prostitution were probably true of some places and not with others, as was the case with concert saloons. But Mc Cabe claimed that they were among the most notorious centers of prostitution in the city, though, indeed, concert saloons were not far behind, and prostitutes "were everywhere, watching for the unwary." In particular, he says, common street walkers "frequent the dance halls and concert saloons, in fact, every place where they can obtain admission and leave no means untried to lure men into their company. As a rule, they are vicious in the extreme, they drink heavily, and are fearfully diseased." After the Civil War, police noted some 750 prostitutes employed in concert saloons and dance houses, out of a total, they said, of some 3,300 in the city; of course, the police may have assumed that mere employment in one of these institutions by a female meant that she automatically was involved in prostitution.

Still, Mc Cabe warned, "Strangers in the city incur a terrible risk in accompanying street walkers and women they meet at concert and dance halls to their homes. In nine cases out of ten, robbery is certain. Murder is too often the result of such an adventure." He took an especially dim view of the Buckingham, or Buckingham Palace, on West Twenty-seventh Street, one of the better dance houses, and, it seemed to him, a center of prostitution.

Descriptions of some of the relatively more commodious establishments provide a clear sense of the best commercial dance halls to be found around the city from before the Civil War until, in some cases, the turn of the century or later. Mc Cabe describes the Buckingham as rather lavishly appointed but profoundly immoral. The Buckingham was, as the *Police Gazette* pointed out, frequented by "solid business men" and "oceans of young fellows of nobby attire, such as you see at Jerome Park or a billiard match." It was also a favorite of men in New York on business. "There a great many drummers taking country customers about," the *Police Gazette* says. "A young gentleman with an undisguised overcoat and a general get-up that seems to suggest Pittsburgh, Pa., is talking to a pretty brunette in a black silk dress, over which a long gold chain trails like a yellow serpent."[7] What was left to the imagination was the reason why all of them were there – which, if the reformers are to be believed, presumably had little enough to do with dancing.

To Mc Cabe, for instance, the place was interesting but hardly harmless. About it, he writes:

The 'Buckingham' is the handsomest dance house in the city. We enter through a lobby into a bar-room, back of which lies the dance hall. This is a gaudily decorated apartment, two stories in height, with a gallery running around it on a level with the second story. Tables and chairs are scattered about the sides of the first floor, but the central space is kept clear for dancing. The galleries are also provided with tables and chairs. At the back is a dimly-lighted space, fitted up like a garden, where those who desire it may sit and drink, and at the side are a shooting-gallery and a restaurant.[8]

In spite of the fact that it was rather "splendidly decorated," Mc Cabe says, the Buckingham "is but one of the numerous gateways to hell with which New York abounds. Men meet abandoned women there, and accompany them to their homes, risking disease, robbery, and even death. The men come from every segment of society, and ought to know better; the women are universally low caste."[9] Prostitution on the premises is not mentioned, but Mc Cabe speaks ominously if somewhat provocatively of the Buckingham being frequented by "the inmates of neighboring houses of ill-fame and street walkers."

Mc Cabe set a typical moral anecdote in the Buckingham. A man was seeking his sister Dora, who was rumored to be a frequenter of the place. "The young lady came out, while he was speaking, in company with a well-dressed man. Instead of complying with her brother's entreaties, she entered a carriage, with her escort, and drove to the Thirtieth Street Police Station to seek release from her brother's importunities. The brother followed, told to the sergeant the story of his sister's shame, and asked him to keep her there until he could summon her father." The sergeant agreed with the request and the woman's father, "a respectable master carpenter," soon appeared at the station house, confirmed his son's story, and begged his daughter to go home with him:

> She answered him flippantly, and the indignant father cursed her for her sin and would have attacked the man had not the police officers prevented him. The woman was locked up for the night in the station house, and brought before the Jefferson Market Police Court the next morning. The father urged that she be sent to some reformatory establishment but the woman met him with the statement that she was twenty-three years old, beyond legal control, and therefore entitled to choose her own mode of life. Her plea was valid, and the magistrate was unwillingly compelled to discharge her from custody, though he endeavored to persuade her to return to her family.[10]

Dora then left the court room, and "was joined by several flashily dressed women, and departed in high spirits, completely ignoring her relatives."

The Haymarket, on Sixth Avenue below Thirteenth Street, was a popular tourist venue in the years after the war. A profile of the establishment (which finally closed in 1913) from Asbury's *The Gangs of New York* makes it clear what the place looked like, and what – other than dancing – it offered. The former theatre (or in some accounts, public bath) was an unprepossessing three-story brick and frame building, painted yellow. During the day it was uninhabited and rather unattractive. "But with the coming of dusk," Asbury says, "as the performers of Satan's Circus gathered for their nightly promenade of Sixth Avenue, the shutters were removed and lights blaze from every window, while from the huge iron hooks before the main entrance hung a sign, 'Haymarket – Grand Soiree Dansant.'" The price of admission was twenty-five cents, women admitted free. Inside, the galleries and boxes that had extended around three sides of the former pit had been kept, and "off them were built small cubicles in which, at the height of the Haymarket's glory, women habitués danced the cancan and gave exhibitions similar to the French peep shows. The descriptive title of 'circus,' which is now generally applied to such displays in this country is said to have originated in the Haymarket."[11]

The Cremourne (or Cremorne), near Sixth Avenue, was another relatively high-end favorite that featured dancing, and more. An article from the *Police Gazette* was quoted in Edward Van Every's *Sins of New York*. He called the place "built and conducted on the London plan." About the women who worked there, the *Police Gazette* said: "How gracefully they dance, how thoroughly they melt into the music! . . . It is not strange that it should be so. To dance well – to captivate their partners – is part of the business which began with flirtation two blocks away." About the place itself, the reporter said: "On another platform opposite the stage . . . there are drinking and eating parties. The air is bluish with the smoke of cigarettes which men and women both indulge in. No loud talking or laughing. It is decorum itself. At closing, early in the morning, "there is a line of cabs, their lamps lit." At three or four o'clock the street is filled with the rattling of their wheels over the cobblestones, "and virtuous people, turning in their sleep, will say, in a dreamy way, 'The Cremorne's Out.'"[12]

Some of the very worst dance houses, said Mc Cabe, were near the docks in Manhattan. "The buildings," he said, generalizing about them, "are generally out of repair, and have a rickety, dirty appearance. The main entrance leads to a long, narrow hall, the floor of which is well sanded. The walls are ornamented with flashy prints, and the ceiling with colored paper cut in various fantastic shapes. There is a bar at the farther end of the room, which is well stocked with the meanest liquors, and chairs and benches are scattered around."[13]

And of course there were the establishments in the Five Points area of lower Manhattan, which were, if anything, considered even more reprehensible. George Foster in *New York by Gas-Light*, at least, saw them as especially sordid. At Pete Williams' Five Points dance house, he said – and undoubtedly at many others – "probably three quarters of the women assembled here, and who frequent this place, are negresses, of various shades and colors." It was a common complaint. As disgusting as this was to Foster, he goes on to point out that, in general, the black women were far more attractive than the white, who were uniformly "bleary-eyed, idiotic, beastly wretches."

Pete Williams, himself – much to Foster's horror – was a black man and probably cohabited with white women. At least Foster hints at this. "He glories in being a bachelor – although there are something under a dozen 'yellow boys' in the neighborhood who have a very strong resemblance to Pete and for whom he has a particular fondness." Williams' male customers, he says, included, not only sailors, but Bowery Boy types, some of whom were members of "rowdy clubs" or volunteer firemen, whose status was not very high with moralists. All of them could expect to be robbed, if not murdered, by the dissolute females who inhabited the place.

Such dance houses, writes Foster, were also generally the scene of fights and other drunk and disorderly activities, and were often raided by the police. In one that was formerly in Water Street, he writes, there was a dance hall some forty feet by sixty feet in size, tucked away in a cellar beneath a stable, and approached by secret doors known only to habitués. The doors were barred and the room was evacuated at a special signal in case of a police raid. The bar room to which these secret doors led, Foster says, also contained a kind of trap: "Beneath the floor at this spot was a pit some eight to ten feet in depth and partly filled with water. By jerking away a timber supporter, attached to a rope, the other end of which was fastened within convenient reach of the bar-keeper's hand, the whole floor in that corner of the room was converted into a nicely-balanced trap, which a few pounds of weight would instantly upset, precipitating whomsoever was upon it into the pit below."[14]

At the same dance house, Foster says, there was a brothel, featuring "from fifteen to twenty girls, inveigled when drunk or taken while destitute and starving... always kept for the use of customers." In the dance hall itself were two roulette tables and two sweat boxes, a bar, and an orchestra of sorts. The walls were lined with benches for the women who danced with customers. This may well have been a description of John Allen's place. Allen's, in any case, was located at 304 Water Street, near the docks. The owner was well known and considered something of an eccentric, even in a place and period when eccentricity was generally tolerated, even respected, in concert-saloon owners and managers.

Allen had come from a well-to-do family and appeared extremely religious. Three brothers were clergymen, and Allen had also studied for the ministry before becoming the proprietor of a notorious dive. In spite of his background, he was famous as a cut-throat and drunk. All in all, his establishment was no better than the rest – and in most things even several cuts below the average – but he supposedly maintained his piety in spite of everything, closing for prayer meetings with his employees three afternoons a week and filling his dance house with Bibles, hymnals, and religious tracts.

He and several other dive owners ostensibly had been made to see the error of their ways by visiting clergymen, and Allen supposedly closed his dance house, a notorious front for prostitution, in August of 1868. In fact, it came out that Allen and the others had been paid by clergymen to hold religious services, sing hymns, pray, and to say that they had voluntarily offered their premises for prayer meetings. His disloyalty was widely resented by patrons and owners, and his reopened dance house failed a short time after the scheme was revealed.

But places like Allen's were common in the city. It was possible to take one's choice. There were dozens of other dance houses in New York, from the lowest to the most elegant – all of them with dubious reputations.

Harry Hill's was arguably the best-known tourist attraction among the so-called dance houses of New York. It was the model for many imitators in the city and elsewhere – probably, in large part, for the Western saloon, as well as its later motion-picture stereotypes. Unlike most dance houses, Hill's was treated in the Society papers. Most, unlike Hill's, rarely figure in the Society documents to any great extent, because most did not present shows, and the Society concerned itself chiefly with places that offered one or another kind of dramatic, minstrel, or variety entertainment.

Some of the concert saloons, however, permitted dancing, and some of the dance houses had stages and routinely presented variety acts along with social dancing. An undated clipping in the Museum of the City of

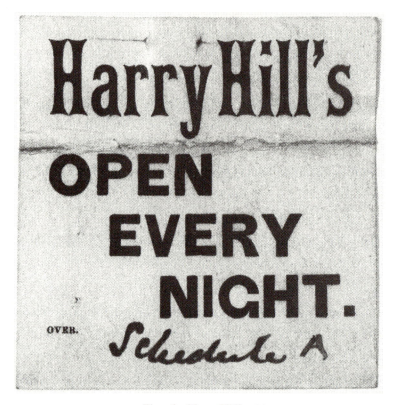

11 Flyer for Harry Hill's, 1887

New York, for example, says that the Winter Garden, a Bowery haunt
where Josh Hart appeared, had both a small stage and a "circular platform
for dancing." The main difference between the two kinds of establishments seems to be in terms of the emphasis – and even that is not consistently reported; a few places, among them Hill's, are sometimes referred
to in documents of the time as dance houses and sometimes as concert
saloons. In fact, they were neither one nor another, but a kind of hybrid
form.

Harry Hill's place, however, was first among equals. A famous establishment on Houston Street near Broadway, remodeled from a house, or
perhaps from a group of old houses, it was widely described by journalists
and others in the late nineteenth century. The place had been founded (no
one is sure of the date; probably it was before the Civil War) by Hill, a
colorful Englishman. About him Herbert Asbury says:

Mr. Hill himself is . . . small, stocky and muscular, a complete type of the pugilist. He keeps the peace of his own concern, and does not hesitate to knock any man down, or throw him out the door, if he breaks the rules of the establishment. He attends to all departments of the trade. He is at the bar; in the hall, where the dancers must be kept on the floor; at the stage, where the low comedies and broad farces are played. He keeps the roughs and bullies in order; he keeps jealous women from tearing out each other's eyes. With burly face and stocky form, he can be seen in all parts of the hall, shouting out, 'Order! Order! Less noise there! Attention! Girls, be quiet!' And these he shouts all evening.[15]

Like Allen, Hill was something of a contradiction in terms – brutal yet flamboyant in his religion. But the difference from Allen appears to have been that he was sincere enough. "Harry Hill," Asbury says, "prided himself on his religious habits, and went to church regularly every Sunday, and to prayer meeting on Wednesday night; and frequently donated large sums to charity, as evidence of his willingness to cooperate in good works." His other enthusiasm was poetry. "Once a week," Asbury wrote, Hill "mounted the stage to give a recital of his output, while the other activities of the resort ceased, not even drinks being served until the master was finished."

A "'letter' from a countryman" which appeared in the *Police Gazette* in 1879, is probably one of the most detailed descriptions of Harry Hill's. It concentrates on the interior of the concert saloon-cum-dance house and what went on there. It begins: "We buy our tickets – twenty-five cents, ladies free – at a little window downstairs." In fact, there were probably separate entrances for men and women; at least Asbury says so. The visitor then entered a bar and proceeded up a flight of stairs to the main dance hall, which had been created by removing the walls of a number of smaller rooms and was decorated overhead with cut paper.

The walls of the room were covered with signs written by Hill in rhyme. "'The pith of these rules,'" says the *Police Gazette*, quoting a contemporary writer, was "no loud talking; no profanity; no obscene or indecent expressions will be allowed; no one drunken, no one violating decency, will be permitted to remain in the room; no man can sit and allow a woman to stand; all men must call for refreshments as soon as they arrive, and the call must be repeated after each dance; if a man does not dance he must leave."[16] In addition, said the *Police Gazette*, " 'No lovers wanted!' is the suggestion from one of the terse wall signs." There is no doubt that Hill's presented entertainment, as well as dancing. "An amusing song or farcical 'nigger' sketch is in progress," said the *Gazette*, "or . . . the Punch and Judy box may

12 Interior of Harry Hill's, *National Police Gazette*, November 22, 1879

be providing amusement. The room is ablaze with light and heavy with smoke." (The Punch and Judy box was a special feature of Hill's main room and is shown in several contemporary illustrations.)

A picture that accompanied the *Police Gazette* article in 1879 illustrates the stage and auditorium. The picture is drawn from a balcony seat (the balcony, divided into separate cubicles, is shown). It also shows a rounded, projecting stage or platform, extending out into the main room of Hill's, with one, perhaps two of what appear to be proscenium doors at floor level, rather than on the stage itself.

A prize fight had already taken place onstage (also not uncommon in nineteenth-century variety theatres). A pit holding nine or ten musicians is in front of the platform, on which a man is shown, presumably performing. Vignettes show a man and woman dancing, two men at a table, drinking with a woman, a prize fight between two females, and two men toasting at the bar. The *Police Gazette* also notes an act on stage that evening. "The stage," the article says, "is occupied by a young lady in a wig the color 'yellow-jack molasses candy,' and a pair of pink tights. Her cheeks are bright with excitement and paint, while each energetic gesture accompanying the topical song she is singing displays her bosom lavishly."

"Singularly enough," adds the article, "Harry Hill's is more discussed and made more of in the country than anywhere else. Hardly a young man comes up to 'York' but takes in Hill's." Indeed, it was something of a New York tourist institution. A flyer tells the out-of-town visitor: "STRANGERS, ask any Hotel Clerk, Policeman, or Conductor, where Harry Hill's is, and they will direct you." And rather imperiously. "If they don't know, they are not fit to hold their position in this great city."

There was little doubt that Hill's, if not an out-and-out house of prostitution, was a popular place for what a later generation would call "pick ups." The *Police Gazette* continues:

> Two such young grangers sit at a table with Charley and I [*sic*], and will have an interesting experience to tell back in Punkton or Rushville of two young ladies in seal-skin saques who sidle down beside them like a couple of birds going to roost.
>
> 'Won't you buy me a drink, dear?' says one. 'You'll treat me, pet, won't you?' remarks the other, and without waiting to discuss the matter further the beautiful creature waves one of the waiter girls, who are flitting about like bees, to the table. Of course. the young men are equal to the occasion, even to standing a treat for the plump little woman who brings on the

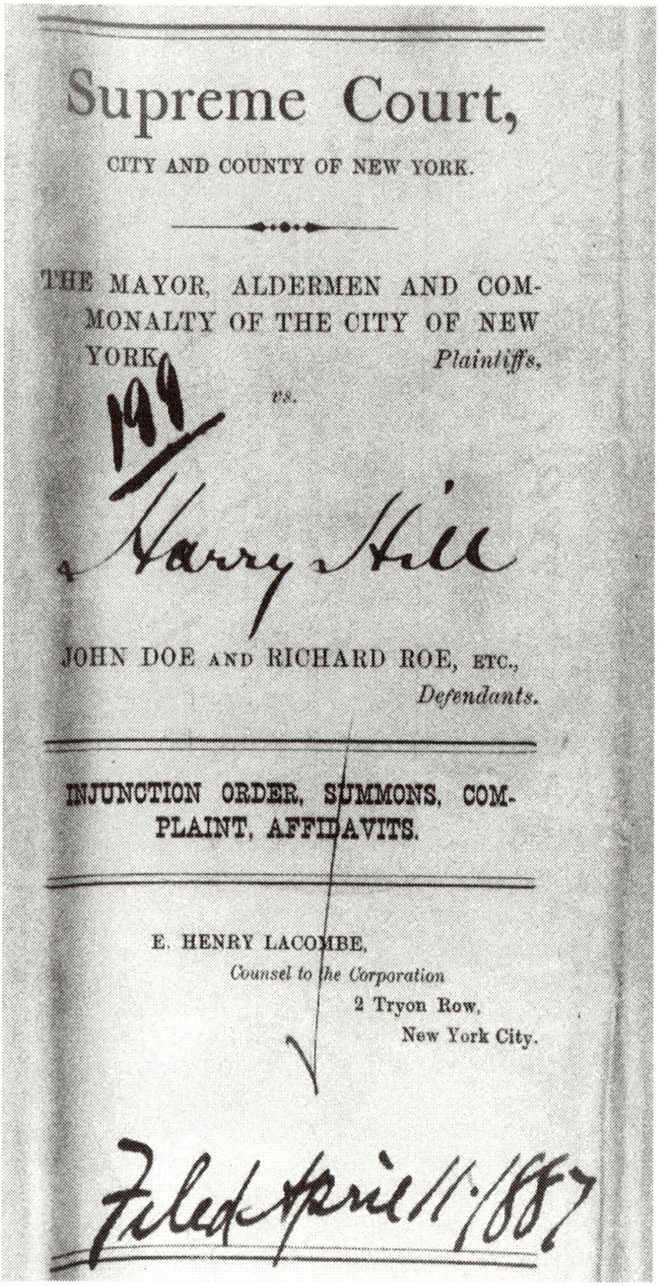

Supreme Court,

CITY AND COUNTY OF NEW YORK.

THE MAYOR, ALDERMEN AND COMMONALTY OF THE CITY OF NEW YORK, *Plaintiffs,*

199

vs.

Harry Hill

JOHN DOE AND RICHARD ROE, ETC., *Defendants.*

INJUNCTION ORDER, SUMMONS, COMPLAINT, AFFIDAVITS.

E. HENRY LACOMBE,
Counsel to the Corporation
2 Tryon Row,
New York City.

Filed April 11. 1887

13 Cover page of a summons issued to Harry Hill's, 1887

14 Supreme Court of New York, "Affidavit of Service," Harry Hill's, 1887 beverages. They get very sociable with the two young ladies, who live in furnished rooms on Crosby Street, and at 2:30 A. M. the four depart in a rather tipsy but orderly condition.[17]

As the *Police Gazette* points out, "The orchestra strikes up and the quadrille begins. The girls dance very nicely (decorously, we might say, if the propriety of this pleasure is conceded), gliding through the figures with genuine grace." Like most such places, however, Hill's saloon was a prime place for fights – which of course were swiftly settled by the owner. "Suddenly there is a crash and a table is upset. One man has struck another in a quarrel about a girl. In any other place there would be quite a little scrimmage. Glasses would be thrown about and the gathering would be in a panic. But not at Harry Hill's. That ubiquitous gentleman [Hill], who has the frame of a pugilist in constant training and a grasp of iron, has already seized the man at fault and conducted him to the stairs, which he finds to his advantage to descend. The dancers hardly pause and the orchestra goes on merrily." In the final analysis, it was the sort of place often replicated throughout the city – though its rivals never gained the attention and free publicity given to Harry Hill's establishment.

Thus, both the beer garden and the dance house influenced the future course of concert saloons, in New York and elsewhere, and were almost certainly influenced by them. Both were related to the concert saloon in one way or another, and both offered models that were useful to concert-saloon proprietors. The German beer garden courted a family audience, producing non-controversial, or only mildly controversial entertainment in a properly sanitized environment. Some concert-saloon owners went in that direction.

On the other hand, many dance houses offered a place where men could indulge fantasies not regularly acceptable in late nineteenth-century New York. Many concert saloons followed suit because such patrons constituted a perennial market. In any event, in the dance house, as in the concert saloon, male patrons were usually provided a special dispensation; it was the women there who were the *real* criminals in the eyes of conservative citizens. Not the men.

Epilogue

They were known as hurdy-gurdy girls, honky-tonk gals, beerjerkers, box rustlers, or pretty waiter girls. Some were prostitutes, but most of them just danced with men for a living.

Richard Erdoes, *Saloons of Old West*, 1979

WITHIN A SHORT TIME AFTER THEIR APPEARANCE IN NEW York City, concert saloons had begun to spread to other urban centers like Baltimore and Washington, and other large cities on the Eastern seaboard. Free or low-cost entertainment had already proved worth the cost – and the trouble – for New York saloons, in spite of the best efforts of the City and the Society for the Reformation of Juvenile Delinquents to stamp it out.

Probably they were an influence on the characteristic "flat floor opera house" so common in the Middle West. These were often "upstairs" entertainment centers – with relatively small stages, flat floors, and sometimes a balcony – which were used both to host traveling professional shows and local amateur events. Although few of their subscribers and builders would have admitted it, the design of the concert saloon – and probably the dance house, too – along with that of halls and other multi-purpose institutions, were influences.

At length, a version of the concert saloon spread to the far West, where it achieved an immense popularity in what was essentially a male-dominated society that depended heavily on saloon life and all that went with it. On October 13, 1877, Frank Leslie's *Illustrated Newspaper* described a Cheyenne, Wyoming, concert saloon in detail. The building might just as easily have appeared on the Bowery or in one of the other cheap entertainment districts in New York City. The street on which the place was built did not resemble the "effete East" in most ways, the writer said. But the interior clearly *did*.

15 Interior of a Cheyenne concert saloon, *Frank Leslie's Illustrated Newspaper*, October 13, 1877

A gambler owned both places, the larger of which was connected to his gambling room, and was described in the article. Only men went there as customers, said the author. They regularly passed back and forth, between the so-called bar and the gambling hall next-door. A flight of stairs in the "bar" led upwards past what in the Eastern theatre would be the dress circle; but in the Cheyenne house is "a single tier of small boxes, open at the back upon a brightly lighted passage." Waiter girls served drinks to men in the boxes from a small bar on the landing; a sign on the stairs urged, "Gents, Be Liberal." The room was narrow and the boxes were close to those across from them. The area below was not the conventional "horseshoe" shape of an ordinary theatre, but funnel-shaped, with the wide end terminating in a stage. The house was painted "barbaric red and yellow" and the walls were crammed with "bizarre Venuses and Psyches." On the stage – or rather, on the stage and in front of it – was a female acrobat:

> The trapeze, through which the wonderful Mlle. Somebody is flying and frisking like a bird, are all swung from the stage to the back of the house,

so that her silken tights and spangles whisk past within a hand's-breadth
of the admiring audience, who can exchange civilities, or even confidences
in her aerial flight.

Below her "the floor is dotted with round tables and darkened with a sea
of hats" and a dense fog of cigar smoke. The orchestra plays, liquor glasses
clink, and patrons talk and "cheer on the performers with liberal enthusiasm." The bar and show helped support the gambling hall, much like
the "show rooms" in a modern Las Vegas or Atlantic City casino. But, all
in all, the establishment was not very different from concert saloons in the
East.

A very large number of Western concert saloons promoted gambling,
which was tolerated and was indeed a fact of life in most frontier towns.
Many Western saloons also promoted the charms of the women who were
employed there – in whatever capacity. One advertisement quoted by Erdoes
begins somewhat ambiguously:

AT THE BELLA UNION
You will Find
PLAIN TALK AND BEAUTIFUL GIRLS!
REALLY GIRLY GIRLS!
No Back Numbers, but as Sweet and Charming
Creatures as Ever Escaped a Female
Seminary.
Lovely Tresses! Lovely Lips! Buxom Forms!
at the
BELLA UNION[1]

The options were limitless. A more or less spontaneous drag act appeared
at The Bird Cage, a famous concert saloon in Tombstone, Arizona, in 1881.
As the *Arizona Star* reported, "Shortly after midnight the curtain rang up
on the cancan in all its glory. As the cancan girls retired three men clad in
tights with women's undergarments over them sprang to the stage and vied
with each other in the obscenity of their actions . . . "[2]

Dora Barrett said that, around the turn of the nineteenth century, the various kinds of concert saloons were known in San Francisco as "box houses."
Talking specifically about a local institution called the Olympia that provided both liquor and entertainment, she writes:

Curtained booths . . . partitioned the semi-circular balcony. The booths
resembled those found in restaurants and, in their seclusion, no doubt

leant themselves to trysts. Drinks were served directly to those in these curtained booths, by white-aproned waiters, and it is conceivable the intimate atmosphere of these 'Boxes' spawned and perpetuated executive-secretary relationships . . .

While the balcony had curtained booths, downstairs were tables and chairs, instead of regular theater seats. The Olympia printed a wine list on the back of each program, offering all manner of drinks . . . [3]

Most people are familiar with the concert saloon but are not aware of it. In later years, many box-houses, dance halls or concert saloons were to appear as backgrounds in Western movies. The makers probably drew the inspiration for many elements − as did the original Western establishments themselves. The famous Harry Hill's was almost certainly one of them. The movies generally showed saloons fitted out with tables for gambling and drinks, a balcony around the room (off of which the hero and the villain usually fell), chorus girls dancing on a small stage, and, from time to time, social dancing in an open area in front of the stage. There is a hint of prostitution upstairs. The image is right, but possibly not quite right for the majority of concert saloons. The movies may have presented a kind of hybrid of the concert saloon and the dance house, with touches of Harry Hill's, the corner saloon, the gambling house, and the German beer garden. But they offered at least a taste of the old concert saloon, and created a piece of American mythology.

By the early twentieth century times had certainly changed for good in New York City. The Society for the Reformation of Juvenile Delinquents had gone out of business; juvenile delinquency and prostitution were examined by others, and few in New York cared very much whether saloons − or any other institution, for that matter − offered shows or girls. There were still a few variations of the old concert saloons, but they raised fewer eyebrows around the city. As late as September 9, 1894, the *Herald* profiled The Abbey, which was cut from the same bolt as earlier concert saloons, although its waiters, as in the Cheyenne establishment, were now all male. John F. Reilly, it said, a court officer and the owner, "has a horde of waiters who hand out very small glasses of beer for five cents, participate in stage performances that may be characterized as absurd, and two "'bouncers' to attend to obstreperous men who come in with abandoned women who bring trade to the court officer's resort."

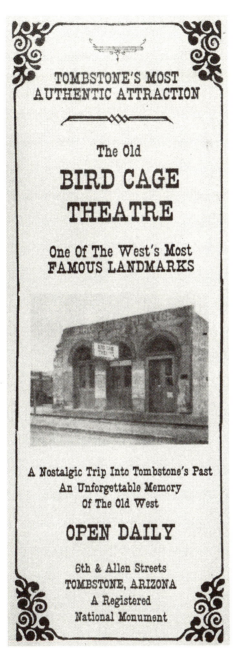

16 Flyer for the extant Bird Cage Theatre, a concert saloon in Tombstone, Arizona.

All the inheritors of the concert-saloon tradition are now dead. Perhaps the last descendant of the era was Sammy's Bowery Follies, a twentieth-century imitation of a Bowery concert saloon employing old entertainers. For years the tour buses lined up in front of Sammy's each night, depositing visitors in search of sanitized Bowery nostalgia. Many of them did not even know what a concert saloon was, but Sammy's appeared "authentic." Meanwhile, the Bowery had changed its character several times – from the cheap entertainment capitol of New York City to a haven for down-and-out alcoholics to – by the 1970s – a haunt of dope addicts. And it was growing too dangerous for tourists. In the early seventies the buses stopped coming. Sammy's Bowery Follies closed, and with it perhaps the last hint of New York's concert saloons.

About the Appendices

Appendix I reproduces the text of the 1872 law, the one mentioned most frequently in the Society for the Reformation of Juvenile Delinquents papers. Appendix II contains a list of popular songs that appeared in concert saloons in New York. The list is compiled from reports of the Society for the Reformation of Juvenile Delinquents. The list is made possible because some of the reports listed by name songs that were sung or played in concert saloons. The year that follows the song title is the year of the report in which it appears, not of the song's publication. Most appeared in concert saloons around the year 1880; it is possible that changes in the Society's rules began to mandate them around that time. Appendix III consists of a similar list of performers who appeared in concert saloons in New York during the same time period. It is also based on the reports of the Society. The years are those of the reports, not of the first appearance of a performer. As with the songs, most names of performers come from around 1880.

Appendix I

Chapter 836

AN ACT to regulate places of public amusement in the City of New York.
[PASSED May 22, 1872, THREE-FIFTHS BEING PRESENT.]
The People of the State of New York, represented in Senate and Assembly do enact as follows:

SECTION 1. It shall not be lawful to exhibit to the public in any building, garden or grounds, concert-room, or other place or room within the City of New York, any interlude, tragedy, comedy, opera, ballet, play, farce, minstrelsy or dancing, or any other entertainment of the stage, or any part or parts therein, or any equestrian, circus, or any performance of jugglers or rope dancing, acrobats, until a license for the place of such exhibition for such purpose shall have been first obtained, as hereinafter provided.

SEC. 2. The Mayor of the City of New York is hereby authorized and empowered to grant such license, to continue in force until the first day of May next ensuing the grant thereof, on receiving for each license so granted, and before issuing thereof, the sum of five hundred dollars; and every manager or proprietor of any such exhibition or performance who shall neglect to take out such license or consent, or cause or allow any such exhibition or performance, or any single one of them, without such license, and every person aiding in such exhibition, and every owner or lessee of any building, part of a building, garden, grounds, concert-room, or other room or place, who shall lease or let the same for the purpose of any such exhibition or performance, or assent that the same be used for any such purpose, except as permitted by such license, and without such license having been previously obtained and then in force, if the same shall be used for such purpose, subjected to a penalty of one hundred dollars for every such exhibition or performance, which penalty the Society for the Reformation of Juvenile

Delinquents in this city is hereby authorized to prosecute, sue for and recover for the use of said Society, in the name of the People of New York.

S E C. 3. The said Mayor is hereby authorized to grant licenses for said exhibitions or performances for any term less than one year, and in any case where such license is for a term of three months or less, the said Mayor is hereby authorized to commute for a sum less than five hundred dollars, but in no case less than two hundred and fifty dollars for a theatre, or one hundred and fifty dollars for a circus, concert-room, or other building or place whatsoever.

S E C. 4. Upon granting every such license authorized by this Act, the said Mayor shall receive from the person to whom the same shall be granted, the amount payable for said license as above provided, which amounts, as respectively received by him, shall be paid over to the Treasurer of the Society for the Reformation of Juvenile Delinquents in the City of New York, for the use of the said Society.

S E C. 5. Any license provided for by this Act may be revoked and annulled by any judge or justice of any Court of Record in said city, upon proof of a violation of any of the provisions of this Act; such proof shall be taken before such judge or justice, upon notice of not less than two days, to show cause why such license should not be revoked; said judge or justice shall hear the proofs and allegations in the case, and determine the same summarily; and no appeal shall be taken from such determination. And any person whose license shall have been revoked or annulled shall not thereafter be entitled to a license under the provision of this Act; on any examination before an officer, pursuant to a notice to show cause, as aforsaid, the accused party may be witness in his own behalf.

S E C. 6. Any person violating any of the provisions of this Act shall be deemed guilty of a misdemeanor, and, upon conviction, shall be punished by imprisonment in the penitentiary, for a term not less than three months nor more than a year, or by a fine no less than one hundred dollars nor more than five hundred dollars, or by both such fine and imprisonment.

S E C. 7. It shall be the duty of every chief of police, sheriff, deputy sheriff, constable, captain of police, policeman, and every other police officer, to enter at any time said places of amusement, and to arrest and convey any person or persons violating any provision of this Act, forthwith, before any police justice, or recorder, or magistrate having jurisdiction in said city, there to be dealt with according to law.

S E C. 8. In case any person shall open, or advertise to open, any theatre, circus, or building, garden or grounds, concert-room, or other place for any such exhibition or performance in said city, without first having obtained a license therefore, as is provided by this Act, it shall and may be lawful for the said Society for the Reformation of Juvenile Delinquents in the said city, to apply to the Supreme Court, or any justice thereof, for an injunction to restrain the opening thereto until he shall have complied with the requitions of this Act in obtaining such license, and also with such order as to costs as such court or justice may deem just and proper to make, which injunction may be allowed, upon a complaint to be in the name of said Society, in the same manner as injunctions are now usually allowed by the practice of said court.

s e c. 9. All acts and parts of acts inconsistent with the provisions of this Act, are hereby repealed.

s e c. 10. This Act shall take place immediately.

STATE OF NEW YORK

OFFICE OF THE SECRETARY OF STATE

I have compared the preceding with the original law on file in this office, and do hereby certify that the same is a correct transcript therefrom, and of the whole of said original law.

Given under my hand and the seal of office, of the Secretary of State, at the city of Albany, this Twenty-seventh day of May, in the year One thousand eight hundred and seventy-two.

ANSON S. WOOD

Dep. Secretary of State

Appendix II

(A list of some of the popular songs sung in institutions called concert saloons, made by the Society for the Reformation of Juvenile Delinquents. Titles are given as they appeared in Society reports. Some songs were performed at several other institutions.)

"Again, Give Me That Loving Glance," Brighton, 1881
"Babies On the Brain," Star and Garter, 1879
"Baby's Gone," Brighton, 1880
"Belles of the Ballet," Old House at Home, 1881
"Blues and the Grays, The," Brighton, 1880
"Boston Mary," Phelps, 1880
"Cat Duet," Winter Garden, 1880
"Cheer Up," Mrs. Riley," Phelps, 1880
"Coming Through the Clover," Phelps, 1880
"Dear Italian Girl," Star and Garter, 1880
"Desire in New Jersey," Elvists', 1880
"Doctor De John's Cod Liver Oil," Elvists', 1880
"Down in the Cotton Field," Bowery Music Hall, 1870
"Duffey's Opening Night," Newport, Year unknown
"Empty the Cradle." Atlantic Garden, 1882
"Fate of the Crew of the Huron," The Garden, 1880
"Finnegan and His Flute," The Garden, 1880
"Fire in the Grate," Sans Souci, 1880
"German Fifth, The," Newport, Year unknown
"Going Back to Ireland to Live," Brighton, 1881
"Golden Wedding, The," Brighton, 1880
"Goodbye, Sweetheart," Phelps, 1880
"Governor' Only Son, The," Star and Garter, 1880
"Green Leaf in Our Bible, The," Old House at Home, 1881
"Hail, Columbia," Ruppert's, 1880

"Heir Convention Show, The," Phelps, 1880
"Help Me Work the Machine," Brighton, 1880
"High Water Pants," The Garden, 1880
"Hump Backed McCarthy," Newport, Year unknown
"Hungry, Starving Boarding House," Newport, Year unknown
"I Am Going Far Away," Newport, Year unknown
"I Don't Believe She Couldn't," Sans Souci, 1881
"I Have No Home," Sans Souci, 1880
"I Love Music, I Love Dancing," Casino, 1882
"I Wish My Ma Was There," Brighton, 1880
"In the Garden Where the Daisys Grow," Newport, Year unknown
"In the Morning By the Bright Light," Bremer Haven, 1881
"Irish Fair, The," Phelps, 1880
"I've Been Too Good a Friend," Sans Souci, 1880
"Kiss Me Again," Fashion, 1881
"Larboard Watch," Newport, 1879
"Little Blue Eyed Maid," Place unknown, Year unknown
"Little Log Cabin on the Hill," Brighton, 1880
"Little Maggie Ann," Brighton, 1880
"Little Pitcher of Beer," Arion, 1879
"Little Widow Dunn," Star and Garter, 1880
"Lover and the Bird, The," Star and Garter, 1881
"Marriage Beds, The," Star and Garter, 1879
"Mary Kelly's Baby," Brighton, 1880
"Mary Kelly's Bear," Sans Souci, 1881
"Mulligan Guard Picnic, The," Sans Souci, 1881
"My Daughter Mary Ann," Resorte Musicale, 1883
"My Dudeen," McHugh's, 1877
"My Mary Ann," Newport, Year unknown
"Nellie, Life of My Home," Brighton, 1880
"Nobody Knows It But Me," Old House at Home, 1881
"Oh, Fred, Tell Them To Stop," Brighton, 1881
"Old Virginia's Shore," Sans Souci, 1881
"On a Stormy Night," Brighton, 1880
"Order of the Full Moon," Phelps, 1880
"Our Boarding House," Resorte Musicale, 1881
"Put On the Golden Glove," Sans Souci, 1881
"Quiet Life for Me, A" Phelps, 1880
"Sally in Our Alley," Sans Souci, 1879
"Scotch Lassie Jean," Fashion, 1881
"Silver Threads Among the Gold," Sans Souci, 1881
"Skids Are Out Today, The," Arion, 1879

"Take This Letter To My Mother," Bremer Haven, 1881

"The Old Home Is Not What It Used to Be," Sans Souci, 1881

"Thou Art So Near and Yet So Far," Star and Garter, 1880

"Turn Off the Gas at the Meter," Star and Garter, 1879

"Twenty Years Ago," Elvists', 1880

"Twilight in the Park," Casino, 1882

"Up in Jones' Woods," The Garden, 1880

"Violets from Mother's Grave," Brighton, 1880

"Way Down Upon the Swanee River," Ruppert's, 1882

"Way Up in Dulkey's Grove," Place unknown, Year unknown

"Wedding Bells Are Ringing," Brighton, 1880

"We March Behind the Band," Place unknown, Year unknown

"What Are the Wild Waves Saying?," Place unknown, Year unknown

"When Jack Comes Over Again," Resorte Musicale, 1881

"When the Robins Nest Again," Resorte Musicale, 1881"

"Where Was Moses When the Lights Went Out?," Phelps, 1880

"Whist! Whist! Whist!," Brighton, 1880

"Yankee Doodle," Ruppert's, 1882

"You Say You Love the Shamrock So Green," Old House at Home, 1881

Appendix III

(A list of some of the singers and other performers appearing in institutions called concert saloons by the Society for Reformation of Juvenile Delinquents. Often only the last name of the performer is given; in that case, a blank substitutes for the first name. Some performers also played at more than one institution. Musicians who did only orchestral work are not listed.)

Binter, James, Levy's Concert Room, 1883
Brand, William, Levy's Concert Room, 1883
Bunnel, Sam, Levy's Concert Room, 1883
Bush, Frank, Fashion, 1880
Butler, Tom, Fashion, 1881
Carran, Jerry, Old House at Home, 1881
Conroy, Jack, Newport, 1879
Curley, Jerry, Old House at Home, 1881
Davenport, _____, Brighton, 1880
Devlin, ("Master"; apparently a child performer), Levy's Concert Room, 1883
Emerson, Billy, Elvists', 1880
Farrell, Bob, Old House at Home, 1881
Goff, _____, Newport, 1879
Gremmel, _____, Star and Garter, 1879
Hill, Raphael, Winter Garden, 1880
Hyland, Chris, Arion, 1879
Lavendorfer, Charles, Levy's Concert Room, 1883
Lawrence (Master), Brighton, 1880
Lorenberg family, Winter Garden, 1881
McCauly, _____, Mc Hugh, 1877
Major, _____, Newport, 1880
Mamina, _____, The Garden, 1880

Mason, Charles, Newport, 1879
Morton, Charles, Resorte Musicale, 1883
Motton, _____, Old House at Home, 1881
O'Halloran, ____, Elvists', 1881
O' Neill, James, Newport, 1879
Roach, Johnny, London Music Hall, 1879
Rose, _____, McHugh, 1877
Russell, _____, Arion, 1879
Russell, Frank, Arion, 1879
Smith, _____, Star and Garter, 1879
Smith, Leo, Newport, 1879
Sukee, _____, Star and Garter, 1879
Tennyson, _____, Newport, 1879
"Uncle Josh," Levy's Concert Room, 1879
Vandermere, Harry, Resorte Musicale, 1883
Victoria (Mlle.), Winter Garden, 1880
Waters, Charles, Levy's Concert Room, 1879
Weaver, Dan, Levy's Concert Room, 1883
Westen, _____, Elvists', 1880

Notes

These notes focus on lengthy quotations used in the book, not otherwise identified in the text. Many of the items come from one of my major sources. The papers filed by the Society for the Prevention of Juvenile Delinquency are abbreviated here, when they appear, as SPJD. (The SPJD documents are brief; there are no page numbers.) The New York *Clipper*, when it appears, *is abbreviated as NYC*. These two references are discussed at length in the Preface. All works used in the preparation of this book or that provide helpful information about the concert saloon are noted in the Bibliography.

Prologue: sources of the concert saloon and its shows

1. New York *Post*, January 2, 1862.
2. M. B. Leavitt, *Fifty Years in Theatrical Management* (New York: Broadway Publishing Company, 1912), p. 48.

1 Where the Devil's work is done: New York City concert saloons during the Civil War era

1. Lloyd Morris, *Incredible New York* (New York: Bonanza Books, 1951), p. 36.
2. Reprinted in Frank Oppel (ed.), *Gaslight New York Revisited* (Secaucus, NJ: Castle Books, 1989), p. 33.
3. Leavitt, *Fifty Years in Theatrical Management*, p. 81.
4. George C. D. Odell, *Annals of the New York Stage*, VII (New York: Columbia University Press, 1931), p. 433.
5. Quoted in William Slout (ed.), *Broadway Below the Sidewalk: Concert Saloons of Old New York* (San Bernardino, California: The Borgo Press, 1994), p. xii.
6. *NYC*, January 2, 1864.
7. Alan Neilson, *The Great Victorian Sacrilege* (Jefferson, NC and London, 1991), p. 127.
8. *NYC*, February 13, 1864.
9. In Slout, *Broadway Below the Sidewalk*, pp. 85–86.

2 Changes in direction: the concert saloon after the war

1. Parker Zellers, "Cradle of Variety: The Concert Saloon" (*Educational Theatre Journal* 20, December 1968), p. 581.

2. SPJD form, January 19, 1884.
3. SPJD form, December 29, 1883.
4. Quoted in Slout, *Broadway Below the Sidewalk*, p. 97.
5. Dora Barrett (with Rose Cordeiro Miller), *My First Love Wears Two Masks* (EL Cerrito, California: Seaview Press, 1981), p. 45.
6. SPJD form, September 15, 1882.

3 Concert-saloon acts

1. *NYC*, February 13, 1864.
2. *NYC*, January 30, 1864.
3. *NYC*, Febuary 27, 1864.
4. *NYC*, January 30, 1864.
5. *NYC*, March 19, 1864.
6. *NYC*, February 6, 1864.
7. SPJD file, September 18, 1875.
8. SPJD file, February 6, 1880.
9. Dora Barrett (with Rose Miller), *My First Love Wears Two Masks*, p. 47.
10. Ibid., p. 46.
11. E.g. SPJD files, November 1, 1876 to May 17, 1877.
12. SPJD file November 1, 1876.

4 Concert saloons: spaces and equipment

1. *NYC*, February 6, 1864.
2. *NYC*, April 23, 1864.
3. Attachment, SPJD file, program, Brighton Winter Garden, date unknown.
4. *NYC*, February 13, 1864.
5. *NYC*, April 9, 1864.
6. *NYC*, April 23, 1864.
7. *NYC*, February 27, 1864.
8. *NYC*, March 19, 1864.
9. *NYC*, February 27, 1864.
10. *NYC*, February 6, 1864.
11. Deposition John Maier, June 13, 1877.
12. Deposition, Owen Geohegan, December 3, 1881.
13. Deposition, William Schwab, April 10, 1884.
14. Ibid.
15. SPJD forms, 1874–1884.
16. *NYC*, March 5, 1864.
17. *NYC*, January 16, 1864.
18. *NYC*, February 20, 1864.

5 Employees and patrons of the concert saloon

1. SPJD file, December 11, 1875.
2. Herbert Asbury, *The Gangs of New York*, (Garden City, NY, Garden City Publishing Company, 1927), p. 346.
3. *NYC*, January 16, 1864.
4. Reprinted in Slout, *Broadway Below the Sidewalk*, pp. 88, 89.
5. Reprinted in ibid., pp. 86–87.
6. Reprinted in Bayrd Still (ed.), *Mirror for Gotham* (New York: New York University Press, 1956), p. 199.
7. *NYC*, April 9, 1864.
8. Reprinted in Still, *Mirror for Gotham*, p. 199.
9. *NYC*, April 23, 1864.
10. *NYC*, January 2, 1864.
11. *NYC*, April 16, 1864.
12. *NYC*, March 5, 1864.
13. Marilyn Hill Wood, *Their Sisters' Keepers: Prostitution in New York, 1830–1870* (Berkeley: University of California Press, 1993), p. 207.
14. Reprinted in Slout, *Broadway Below the Sidewalk*, pp. 87–88.
15. Reprinted in ibid., p. 88.
16. *NYC*, February 13, 1864.
17. *NYC*, March 19, 1864.
18. *NYC*, January 2, 1864.

6 Related forms

1. James Mc Cabe, Jr., *New York By Gaslight*, reprint of *New York by Sunlight and Gaslight* (New York: Greenwich House, 1984), pp. 643–644.
2. J. Ralph, "The Bowery," *Century Magazine*, December, 1891, p. 236.
3. James Mc Cabe, *Lights and Shadows of New York Life* (Philadelphia: National Publishing Company, 1872), p. 551.
4. Ralph, "The Bowery," p. 236.
5. Mc Cabe, *Lights and Shadows of New York Life*, p. 553.
6. Ralph, "The Bowery," p. 236.
7. Quoted in Edward Van Every (ed.), *Sins of New York* (New York: Benjamin Blom. 1972), p. 191.
8. Mc Cabe, *New York By Gaslight*, p. 490.
9. Ibid.
10. Ibid., p. 486.
11. Asbury, *The Gangs of New York*, p. 178.
12. Quoted in ibid., p. 180.
13. Mc Cabe, *Lights and Shadows of New York Life*, p. 597.
14. George G. Foster, *New York by Gas-Light and Other Urban Sketches*. Ed. Stuart Blumin (Berkeley: University of California Press, 1990), pp. 146–147.
15. Asbury, *The Gangs of New York*, p. 183.
16. Ibid.
17. Quoted in Van Every, *Sins of New York*, pp. 201–202.

Epilogue

1. Quoted in Richard Erdoes, *Saloons of the Old West* (New York: Gramercy Books, 1979), p. 172.
2. Ibid.
3. Barrett, *My First Love Wears Two Masks*, pp. 42–43.

Bibliography

The chief sources for this book – the Society papers and the *Clipper* articles – are discussed at length in the Preface, together with a number of other books, articles, and manuscripts that were particularly useful to me, especially the Mc Cabe guides. All of them may be found below. But additional works were helpful in some way in the preparation of this book or in tracing the history of the concert saloon, and its American ancestors and descendants. These books also are listed below:

Allen, Robert. *Horrible Prettiness.* Chapel Hill: University of North Carolina Press, 1991.

Aldrich, Elizabeth. *From the Ballroom to Hell: Grace and Folly in Nineteenth-Century Dance.* Evanston: Northwestern University Press, 1991.

Anderson, Ann. *Snake Oil, Hustlers and Hambones: The American Medicine Show.* Jefferson, North Carolina: McFarland and Co., 2000.

Applebaum, Stanley, editor. *Show Songs from "The Black Crook" to "The Red Mill."* New York: Dover Publications, Inc., n.d.

Aquila, Richard, editor. *Wanted Dead or Alive: The American West in Popular Culture.* Urbana: University of Illinois Press, 1996.

Armstrong, David and Elizabeth Metzger Armstrong. *The Great American Medicine Show.* New York: Prentice-Hall, 1991.

Asbury, Herbert. *The Barbary Coast.* New York: Alfred A. Knopf, 1933.

The Gangs of New York. Garden City, New York: Garden City Publishing Co., Inc., 1927.

Bahr, Howard M. *Skid Row.* New York: Oxford University Press, 1973.

Bailey, Peter. *Popular Culture and Performance in the Victorian City.* Cambridge: Cambridge University Press, 1998.

editor. *Music Hall: The Business of Pleasure.* Milton Keynes, UK: Open University Press, 1986.

Barrett, Dora (with Rose Cordeiro Miller). *My First Love Wears Two Masks.* El Cerrito, California: Seaview Press, 1981.

Barth, Gunther. *City People.* New York: Oxford University Press, 1982.

Bean, Annamarie, James V. Hatch, Brooks McNamara, editors. *Inside the Minstrel Mask: Readings in Nineteenth-Century Blackface Minstrelsy.* Hanover, NH: Wesleyan University Press, and University Press of New England, 1996.

Bogden, Robert. *Freak Show: Presenting Human Oddities for Amusement and Profit.* Chicago: University of Chicago Press, 1998.

Bogue, Donald J. *Skid Row in American Cities.* Chicago: Community and Family Study Center, 1963.

Bratton, J. S., editor. *Music Hall: Performance & Style.* Milton Keynes, UK and Philadelphia: Open University Press, 1986.

Bristow, Eugene Kerr. "Look Out for Saturday Night: A Social History of Professional Variety Theatre in Memphis, Tennessee, 1859–1880." Ph.D. Dissertation, University of Iowa, 1957.

Brown, Henry Collins, editor. *Valentine's Manual of Old New York, 1927.* New York: Valentine's Manual, Inc., 1926.

Brownlow, Kevin. *The War, the West, and the Wilderness.* New York: Alfred A. Knopf, 1979.

Butsch, Richard. *The Making of American Audiences: From Stage to Television.* New York and Cambridge: Cambridge University Press, 2000.

    editor. *For Fun and Profit: The Transformation of Leisure into Consumption.* Philadelpia: Temple University Press, 1990.

Calkins, Raymond. *Substitutes for the Saloon: An Investigation for the Committee of Fifty.* Boston: Houghton Mifflin, 1901.

Cockrell, Dale. *Demons of Disorder: Early Blackface Minstrels and Their World.* New York and Cambridge: Cambridge University Press, 1997.

Culhane, John. *The American Circus: An Illustrated History.* New York: Henry Holt, 1990.

Cullen, Jim. *The Civil War in Popular Culture.* Washington, DC: Smithsonian Institution Press, 1995.

Dallas, Sandra. *No More Than Five in a Bed: Colorado Hotels of the Old Days.* Norman: University of Oklahoma Press, 1967.

Dary, David. *Seeking Pleasure in the Old West.* New York: Knopf (paperback edition), University Press of Kansas, 1997.

Delgado, Alan. *Victorian Entertainment.* New York: American Heritage Press, 1971.

Dennett, Andrea. *Weird and Wonderful: The Dime Museum in America.* New York: New York University Press, 1997.

Duis, Perry. *The Saloon: Public Drinking in Chicago and Boston, 1880–1920.* Urbana: University of Illnois Press, 1983.

Dykstra, Robert. *The Cattle Towns: A Social History of the Kansas Cattle Trading Centers, 1867–1885.* New York: Alfred A. Knopf, 1968.

Elliot, Eugene. *History of Variety-Vaudeville from the Beginning to 1914.* Seattle: University of Washington Press, 1941.

Ellis, David M., et al. *A Short History of New York State.* Ithaca: Cornell University Press, 1957.

Erdoes, Richard. *Saloons of the Old West.* New York: Gramercy Books, 1979.

Erenberg, Lewis. *Steppin' Out: Nightlife and the Transformation of American Culture.* Westport, CT: Greenwood Press, 1981.

Ernst, Alice Henson. *Trouping in the Oregon Country: A History of Frontier Theatre.* 1961. Reprint. Westport, CT: Greenwood Press, 1974.

Foster George. *New York By Gas-Light.* Berkeley: University of California Press, 1990.

Fremont, Robert A., editor. *Favorite Songs of the Nineties*. New York: Dover Publications, Inc., 1973.

Garrett, Thomas M., "A History of Pleasure Gardens in New York City, 1700–1865." Ph.D. Dissertation, New York University, 1978.

Gavin, James. *Intimate Nights: The Golden Age of New York Cabaret*. New York: Grove Weidenfeld, 1991.

Gilbert, Douglas. *American Vaudeville*. New York: Dover Publications, 1963.

Gilfoyle, Timothy. *City of Eros: New York, Prostitution, and the Commercialization of Sex, 1790–1920*. New York: Norton, 1992.

Grafton, John, editor. *New York in the Nineteenth Century*. New York: Dover Publications, 1977.

Grover, Kathryn, editor. *Hard at Play: Leisure in America, 1840–1940*. Amherst: University of Massachusetts Press, 1992.

Halttunen, Karen. *Confidence Men and Painted Women: A Study of Middle-Class Culture in America, 1830–1870*. New Haven: Yale University Press, 1982.

Henderson, Mary. *The City and the Theatre*. Clifton, NJ: James T. White and Company, 1973.

Hill, Marilyn Wood. *Their Sisters' Keepers: Prostitution in New York City, 1830–1870*. Berkeley: University of California Press, 1993.

Hoh, LaVahn G., and William H. Rough. *Step Right Up! The Adventure of Circus in America*. White Hall, VA: Betterway Publications, 1990.

Jackson, Kenneth, editor. *The Encyclopedia of New York City*. New Haven and New York: Yale University Press and the New-York Historical Society, 1995.

Jennings, John J. *Theatrical and Circus Life: or, Secrets of the Stage, Greenroom and Sawdust Arena*. St. Louis: Herbert and Cole, 1882.

Kibler, M. Alison. *Rank Ladies: Gender and Cultural History in American Vaudeville*. Chapel Hill: University of North Carolina Press, 1999.

Kift, Dagmar. *The Victorian Music Hall: Culture, Class, and Conflict*. Cambridge and New York: Cambridge University Press, 1996.

Koon, Helen Wickham. *Gold Rush Performers*. Jefferson, NC: McFarland, 1994.

Lankevich, George and Howard B. Furer. *A Brief History of New York City*. Port Washington, New York: Associated Faculty Press, Inc., 1984.

Leavitt, M. B. *Fifty Years in Theatrical Management*. New York: Broadway Publishing Company, 1912.

Leman, Walter. *Memories of an Old Actor*. San Francisco: A. Roman, 1886.

Levine, Lawrence. *Highbrow Lowbrow: The Emergence of Cultural Hierarchy in America*. Cambridge, MA: Harvard University Press, 1988.

Lhamon, W. T., Jr. *Raising Cain: Blackface Performance from Jim Crow to Hip Hop*. Cambridge: Harvard University Press, 1998.

Logan, Olive. *Before the Footlights and Behind the Scenes*. Philadelphia: Parmalee and Company, 1870.

Lott, Eric. *Love and Theft: Blackface Minstrely and the American Working Class*. New York: Oxford University Press, 1993.

Mc Cabe, James D. Jr. [Edward Winslow Martin], *Lights and Shadows of New York Life, or, Sights and Sensations of the Great City*. Philadelphia: National Publishing Company, 1872.

New York By Gaslight [originally published as *New York by Sunlight and Gaslight*, 1882]. New York: Greenwich House, 1984.

McMinn, George. *Theater of the Golden Age in California.* Caldwell Idaho: Caxton Printers, 1941.

McNamara, Brooks. "'A Congress of Wonders': The Rise and Fall of the Dime Museum." *Emerson Society Quarterly* 20 (3rd quarter 1974): 216–232.

Step Right Up. Revised edition. Jackson: University Press of Mississippi, 1995.

Day of Jubilee: The Great Age of Celebrations in New York, 1788–1909. New Brunswick, NJ: Rutgers University Press, 1997.

Mahar, William J. *Behind the Burnt Cork Mask: Early Blackface Minstrelsy and Antebellum American Popular Culture.* Urbana: University of Illinois Press, 1999.

Mankowitz, Wolf. *The Lives, Loves, and Legends of Adah Issacs Menken.* New York: Stein and Day, 1982.

Mattfield, Julius, editor. *'Variety' Music Cavalcade.* New York: Prentice-Hall, 1952.

Moody, Richard. *Ned Harrigan.* Chicago: Nelson-Hall, 1980.

Morris, Lloyd. *Incredible New York.* New York: Bonanza Books, 1951.

Nadel, Stanley. *Little Germany.* Urbana: University of Illinois Press, 1990.

Nasaw, David. *Going Out: The Rise and Fall of Public Amusements.* New York: Basic Books, 1990.

Nielsen, Alan. *The Great Victorian Sacrilege.* Jefferson, North Carolina and London: McFarland and Company, 1991.

O'Conner, Richard. *Hell's Kitchen.* New York: Old Town Books, 1993.

Odell, George C. D. *Annals of the New York Stage.* 15 volumes. New York: Columbia University Press, 1927–1949.

Oppel, Frank, editor. *Gaslight New York Revisited.* Secaucus, NJ: Castle Books, 1989.

Ormsby, Ted. *Subduing Satan.* Chapel Hill: University of North Carolina Press, 1990.

Peiss, Kathy. *Cheap Amusements: Working Women and Leisure in Turn-of-the-Century New York.* Philadelphia: Temple University Press, 1986.

Powers, Madelon. *Faces Along the Bar.* Chicago: The University of Chicago Press, 1998.

Quennel, Peter. *London's Underworld.* London: Spring Books, 1950.

Ralph, J. "The Bowery" *Century Magazine* (December 1891): 236.

Root, Deane L. *American Popular Stage Music, 1860–1880.* Ann Arbor, Michigan: UMI Research Press, 1981.

Sante, Luc. *Low Life.* New York: Ferrar, Straus, Giroux, 1991.

Shapiro, Ann-Louise. "Working Girls." *International Labor and Working Class History* 45 (Spring 1994): 96–107.

Slout, William, editor. *Broadway Below the Sidewalk: Concert Saloons of Old New York.* San Bernadino, CA: The Borgo Press, 1994.

editor. *Popular Amusements in Horse and Buggy America.* San Bernadino, CA: The Borgo Press, 1995.

editor. *Life Upon the Wicked Stage.* San Bernadino, CA: The Borgo Press, 1996.

Smith, Gene and Jayne Barry, editors. *The Police Gazette.* New York: Simon and Schuster, n.d.

Smith, Matthew Hale. *Sunshine and Shadow in New York.* Hartford: J. B. Burr, 1869.

Snyder, Robert W. *The Voice of the City: Vaudeville amd Popular Culture in New York.* New York: Oxford University Press, 1989.

Sonneck, O. G. *Early Concert Life in America*. Leipzig: Breitkopf and Hartel, 1907.
Stein, Charles W. *American Vaudeville As Seen By Its Contemporaries*. New York: Alfred
    A. Knopf, 1984.
Still, Bayrd, editor. *Mirror for Gotham*. New York: New York University Press, 1956.
Todd, Charles Burr. *The Story of the City of New York*. New York: G. P. Putnam's Sons,
    1888.
Toll, Robert. *Blacking Up*. New York: Oxford University Press, 1974.
Van Every, Edward, editor. *Sins of New York*. New York: Benjamin Blom, Inc., 1972.
Walkowitz, Judith. *City of Dreadful Delights*. Chicago: The University of Chicago Press,
    1992.
Watson, Margaret G. *Silver Theatre: Amusements of Mining Frontier, 1850–1864*.
    Glendale, California: The Arthur Clark Company, 1965.
Wilmeth, Don B. *American and English Popular Entertainment: A Guide to Information
    Sources*. Detroit: Gale Research Company, 1980.
Wroth, Warwick and Arthur Edgar Wroth. *The London Pleasure Gardens in the Eighteenth
    Century*, 1896. Reprint. Hampden, Connecticut: Shoestring Press, 1979.
Zellers, Parker. "The Cradle of Variety: The Concert Saloon." *Educational Theatre
    Journal* 20 (December 1968): 578–585.
    Tony Pastor: Dean of the Vaudeville Stage. Ypsilanti, Michigan: Eastern University
    Press, 1971.

Index

NOTE: The Society for the Prevention of Juvenile Delinquency is abbreviated to SPJD.

Abbey, The 120
Abe, the Pioneer, or the Mad Hunter of Arizona
    (melodrama) 39
Academy of Fun, The 48, 56, 63
acrobats 16, 31, 48, 54, 118–19
Actors' Fund 28
acts 41–60
    as advertising device 29, 59, 76
    ethnic performers 4–5, 79–80
    and immorality charges 2, 12, 17–18, 20
    professional 49–50, 77–8, 117, 130–1
    range before Concert Bill 15–16
    SPJD documents on 57–60, 130–1
    see also acrobats; child actors; circus; dance
        acts; drag acts; magic acts; minstrelsy;
        musical entertainments; puppet shows;
        sketches; songs; women (performers); *and*
        under beer gardens, German; dance
        houses; variety theatre
advertising xiii, 9, 62–4
    of "bar maids" 31
    entertainments as 26, 59, 76
    handbills 62, *110*
    medicine shows and xiii, 9, 33
    in newspapers 28, 37, 42, 62
    sandwich boards 62
    signs 63–4, 107
    stock poster *71, 72*
    transparencies 25, 62–3
African Americans 79–80
afterpieces 6–7, 57
alcohol
    in German beer gardens 96, 99
    and immorality 2, 12, 17–18, 20
    post-war decline in concern over 26
    sale as main business of concert saloons 26,
        41, 59, 76, 86

temperance and abstinence
    movements 12
    in theatres 20–1, 35
Alhambra Theatre 39
Allen, John 109
Allen, Robert C. xix. 3
Allen, William ("Billy") 43, 66, 81
amateur performances 32–3, 117
American Concert Hall 28
American Hall 49
amusement parks 9
Arion 128, 130, 131
Arizona Star 119
Asbury, Herbert xvi, xx, 82, 107, 110–11
"Asmodeus" 75, 81, 85, 86
Assembly 23–4
assignations 25, 83, 119–20
Athenaeum 585, 37, 39
Atlantic Garden 27, *100*, 101–3, 104, 127
Audran, Edmond 36

Bailey, James 8
Baker's Central Hall 33
balconies
    concert saloons 73–4, 76
    dance houses 106, 107, *112*, 113
    flat floor opera houses 117
    German beer gardens *98*, 102
    San Francisco box houses 119–20
Ballard's What Is It 42, 61, 63, 75, 90, 92
ballet girls 20, 85
Baltimore 77, 117
bar maids 31
Barnum, P. T. 8
Barrett, Dora 37, 56–7, 119–20
bartenders *71, 72*, 81
Batchelor's Music Hall 48, 49, 54

beer gardens, German xi, xv, xvii, xviii,
    96–104
  acts 39–40, 50, 99, 101, 102, 103, 104
  family orientation 25, 27–8, 96, 99, 101,
    103, 104, 116
  gambling 99, 101
  matinees 28
  music 50, 99, 102, 103, 104
  non-German-speaking patrons and acts 27,
    101, 102, 104
  shooting halls 102
  SPJD investigations of xv, 29, 31–2
  spaces and equipment 98, 99, 101, 102
  summer gardens 75, 99
  Sunday opening 99, 101
Bella Union 119
Belles of the Concert Saloon (1862 publication)
    19, 84
benefit shows 29, 54, 82
Bigelow, Charlie 33–4
Bijou Opera House 36
Billboard magazine xiv
billiards 12, 74
bills, legislative
  of 1839 22
  of 1872 23–4, 28–9, 48, 49, 124–6;
    amendment, 1875 and 1876 xv,
    xvi–xvii
  see also Blue Laws; Concert Bill
Binter, James 130
Bird Cage, Tombstone, Arizona 119, *121*
black Americans 56, 79–80, 94, 108
  minstrel troupes xvii, 7, 80
black and "black-and-tan" saloons 79
Black Crook, The (musical play) 5, 12, 72
blackface performers *see* minstrelsy
Blue Laws 62, 89
Blythe's String Band 42
Bon Ton 24–5, 42, 64–5, 71, 94, 94
"Bones" (minstrel role) 6, 30
Booth's Theatre 35
Boulevard 24, 80, 81, 85, 88, 93
Bowery *13*
  changing character 99, 122
  concert saloons xi, 1, 2, 11, 12–13, *13*
  dime museums 8, 12, 97
  German immigrants 97, 101
  theatres 36
Bowery Boy types 108
Bowery Concert Hall (*later* Melodeon) 15
Bowery Garden Theatre 39
Bowery Mission and Home for Young Men 13
Bowery Music Hall, The 48, 52, 82, 127
Bowery Theatre 97
Bowery Varieties, The 30–1

box houses 119, 120
boxes 74
  in dance houses 107
  private 1, 31, 64, 65, 74
  in West 74, 118, *118*, 119–20
boxing matches 54
Brand, William 59, 130
Bremer Haven 62, 128, 129
Brighton Winter Garden 48, 50, 64, 71, 130
  songs performed at 127, 128, 129
Britain
  music halls xiii, xvi, 3, *4*, 4–5, 9, 74; masters
    of ceremonies 4, 47
  pleasure gardens xvi, 8
  Theatres Registry Act (1843) 4
British Blondes, The 5–6, 12
Broadway, lower xi, 1, 12, 13–15
Broadway Music Hall 28, 78
Buckingham (Palace) dance house 73, 105–7
Bull's Head Tavern, site of former 101–2, 103
Bunnel, Sam 130
burlesque xi, xiii, 9, 37, 90
  early form xv, 5–6
Burns, Frank 43
Burrows, Edwin G. xix
Burton, Edward 58
Busch, Frank 54, 130
Butler, James 59
Butler, Robert 78
Butler, Tom 62, 130
Butler's Varieties 78
Butsch, Richard xix
Byrne, Charles 29

cabarets 5
cafe concert *and* cafe chantant, French 3–4
calliope, imitations of 47
Canterbury 11, 15–16, 19–20, 23–4, 28, 73
Carran, Jerry 130
Carroll's Sixth Avenue Saloon 57–9, 79–80
Casino 31–2, 51, 73, 128, 129
Centennial Gardens 49, 52, 53, 71
Century 102–3
Champion Music Hall 74, 81, 82, 85, 91–2, 93
charges, admission 26, 64, 65, 70, 101, 107
checks 86
Cheyenne, Wyoming 117–19, *118*
child actors 36, 51, 59, 130
Chinese immigrants, satire on 54
chorus girls, burlesque 5–6
cigar girls 82, 85
cinema 7, 109, 120
circus xiv, 9, 79, 107
  influence on concert saloon 5, 8, 60
  minstrel acts 7, 53

cities, concert saloons in other US xi, 77, 117
Civil War xi, 11–26
    concert saloon before 15
    military in New York during 12, 17, 18, 27,
        40, 91–2, 104
    post-war period xi–xii, 2, 25, 27–40
    slump 16–17
Clark, Jenny 84
Cleveland, Ohio 79
Clinton Garden 49, 52, 54, 71
Clipper xiv–xv, xv–xvi, xvii, 20, 24–5
    on patrons 91–2, 93–4
    on spaces and equipment 65–8
    on waiter girls 85–6, 87–8
    see also individual citations detailed in
        Notes
comedians 15, 37, *38*, 104
Concert Bill (1862) xiv, xvi, 16–18
    effect xv, 18–21, 41, 42, 61–2, 77
    genesis 16–18, 91
    SPJD's receipt of fines under 22–3, 28
concert gardens xii
concert halls 3
concert rooms xii, xvii, 3
Conroy, Jack 130
control, social 22
corruption, civic 61
Cosmopolitan Theatre 36
costumes 5–6, 72–3
country customers 93–4, 105, 111, 113
court papers xv, *114–15*
Cremourne (or Cremorne) dance house 107
Curley, Jerry 130
Current Literature 2
Curtis and Health Minstrel Burlesque
    Company 64

dance acts xvii, 56, 104
dance floors 73, 76
dance houses xiv, xvii–xviii, 96, 104–16
    acts 111, *112*, 113, 116
    fights 116
    gambling 109
    influence on West 117, 120
    patrons 91, 96, 104, 105, 108
    sexuality and prostitution 96, 104, 105,
        106, 108–9, 113–16
    spaces and equipment 106, 107, 110, *112*,
        113
dance tunes 50–1
Dare, Leona 39
Davenport (performer) 130
De Briantio 43
Deutsches Volksgarten 99, 101
Devlin, Master (child actor) 51, 59, 130

dime museums xi, 5, 8, *14*
    Bowery 8, 12, 97
    entertainments 7, 60
    family audience 35
    lecture rooms 29, 35
    transparencies 62
dining rooms, private 66–7
"dives" 3
Dowling, Justice 23–4
drag acts 31, 52, 79, 119
"dragging the town" 9
Dramatic News 29
"Duffy's Opening Night" (song) 55, 127
"Dutch" (German immigrants) 7, 37, 39

elderly patrons 94
Elwists' 55, 62, 127, 129, 130, 131
Emerson, Billy 130
Emmett, Dan 6
employees of concert saloons 77–90
    see also acts; musical entertainments; owners
        and managers; waiter girls; *and under*
        prostitutes
entertainments *see* acts; musical entertainments
equipment *see* spaces and equipment
Erdoes, Richard 117
Essex Hall, Maier's 51, 54, 68, 70
establishment of concert saloons xi, 3
"Ethiopian delineator" (act) 15
ethnic groups
    mixing of 79–80, 94, 108
    performers from 4–5, 79–80
    satire on 7, 53–4, 56, 57
    see also black Americans; German
        Americans; Indians, North American;
        Irish Americans; Jews
Eureka *see* Lee and Hatstatt's Eureka; Shafer's
    Eureka
Evening Post 83, 93

family orientation
    concert saloons develop xix, 9–10, 25, 41,
        60, 104
    dime museums 35
    German beer gardens 25, 27–8, 96, 99, 101,
        103, 104, 116
    matinees 28, 39
    summer gardens 75
Farrell, Bob 130
Fashion, The 53, 54, 128, 130
fights 92, 108, 116
firemen, volunteer 108
fireworks 9
Five Points area 108
Four-forty-four (444) 47

Fourteenth Street Theatre 40
France: cafe concert and cafe chantant 3–4
freak shows 61, 63
free and easys 3
frontier *see* West
"Fun in an Elevated Station" (sketch) 33

Gaieties, The 20, 42, 65
gambling 1, 94, 99, 101, 109, 118, 119
Garden, The 47, 51, 127, 128, 129, 130
gardens
    pleasure xvi, 5, 7, 8–9
    rooftop 75, 104
    summer 75, 99
    winter 99
Gaunt, Percy vi, 12
Geohagan, "Ownie" 54, 63
German Americans
    entertainments for 50, 101
    immigration 96, 97, 102
    performers 80
    satirization 7, 53, 56
    see also beer gardens, German
Geschwandrer, S. 34
Gilbert, Douglas 89
Goebel, Ferdinand 31–2
Goff (performer) 130
Gopnik, Adam 5
Gramercy Hall (O'Donnell's) 49, 53, 55–6, 71, 81
Grand Street, concert saloon at 107 42
Gremmel (performer) 130
Grovesteen (manager of Champion
    Music Hall) 74
gymnastic acts 48, 54, 118–19

halls, rental 29, 33–4
handbills 62, *110*
handicaps, comic stereotyping of 57
Harlem Bridge Concert Garden 27
Harlem Hall 33–4
Harlow, Alvin 90, 103
harmonic evenings 42–3
Harper's New Monthly Magazine 97
Harper's Weekly 14, 15, *98*, 101
Harrigan, Edward, and Anthony Hart
    50, 55
Hart, Josh 110
Hartmann's Theatre 22
Haydon, George 63, 67
Haymarket 107
Hays, Will. S. *44–5*
Healy, John E. 33–4
Hell's Kitchen (*now* Clinton) 15
Helms, Captain 20
Herald, The 15, 19–20, 37, 42, 62, 120

Hill, Harry 111
    court papers served on *114*–15
    dance house 15, 73, 109–16, *110, 112*, 120
Hill, Marilyn Wood xx, 90
Hill, Raphael 130
Hoboken, New Jersey 97
Home Journal 62
homosexuality 78–9, 81
House of Refuge xv
Howard, Al 81
Hoyt, Charles vi, 12
Hubert's Prospect Concert Garden 73
Hyland, Chris 130

"I Have No Home" (song) *45*, 128
Illustrated Newspaper 117–19, *118*
immigrant groups *see* ethnic groups
immorality, charges of 2, 12, 17–18, 20
improvisation 56, 57
Indians, North American 16, 33–4
influences on concert saloon xiii, xv–xvi, 3–9
    see also advertising; burlesque; cafe concert;
        circus; dime museums; minstrelsy; music
        hall, British
Interlocutor 6
Irish Americans
    performers 4–5, 37, 58, 68, 80
    satirization of 7, 53
"Irish Justice" (sketch) 57
itinerant performers 77–8
Ixion (burlesque) 5–6

Jackson's Brass Band 42
Jennings, John J. 35
Jews 53–4, 80, 104
Johnson, "Signora" 78
Johnson, William Henry 61

Karlsbader Ladies Orchestra, World-Famed 32
Kleindeutchland 97
Koster and Bial's cabaret 75

Ladendorfer, Charles 59, 130
"Lady Show, The" 48
Lambert Children (act) 36
Lawrence, Master 130
Leavitt, M. B. xvi, 6, 7, 16–17
lecture rooms, dime museum 29, 35
Lee and Hatstatt's Eureka 24, 46–7, 67, 73, 94
legislation, NY State *see* bills, legislative
Leslie, Frank 117
Levy's Concert Room 51, 59–60, 130, 131
licensing of performances
    bill of 1872 *see under* bills, legislative
    SPJD's investigations 28–40, 60

lighting, stage 72
Lincoln, Abraham 16
Lindenmeyer's Odeon 101
"Little Old Market Woman, The" (song) 43
"Little Pitcher of Beer, A" (song) 50, 128
London, England 4, *4*, 8
London Museum, New York 35
London Music Hall 48, 131
Lorenberg family 130
Lyceum Concert Garden 63–4

Mabille Palace 54
MacIntyre and Heath 56
McArthur, Benjamin 77
Mc Cabe, James Jr xiv, xvi, 6
  on Bon Ton 24–5
  on dance houses 73, 96, 104, 105–7, 107–8
  on fights 92
  on German beer gardens 99, 102, 103
  on patrons 83, 90–1, 92–3
  on waiter girls 1, 16, 83–5
McCauly (performer) 130
McHugh's Free and Easy 49–50, 53, 128, 130, 131
McKay, Charles 88
Madden, Owen ("Ownie") 82
Magar's Concert Hall 101
magic acts 34, 35, 55
magic lantern shows 35
Maier's Essex Hall 51, 54, 68, 70
Major (performer) 130
male-oriented establishments xi, 1, 30–1, 41, 82–3, 96
  decline xix, 9–10, 25, 41, 60, 104
Mamina (performer) 130
Manhattan Elevated Railway 33
Manhattan Hall 33
Marginal Club 82
Mason, Charles 131
Masonic lodge 32
masters of ceremonies 2, 4, 6, 47, 58
matinees 28, 39, 64
Mazeppa 12, 39
medicine shows 29, 57, 72
  and advertising xiii, 9, 33
Melodeon 15, 20, 47, 62–3, 67–8
Menken, Adah Isaacs 12, 39
Metropolitan 47–8
midget minstrel routines 51
military patrons 12, 17, 18, 27, 40, 91–2, 104
minstrelsy xvii, 6–8
  acts in concert saloons 7–8, 30–1, 52–3, 56, 59, 60
  afterpieces 6–7, 57
  amateur 51

black troupes xvii, 7, 80
  and burlesque 6
  in circus 7, 53
  in Civil War 16–17
  dance numbers originating in 51
  decline 52–3, 60
  influence on cs xiii, xv, 5, 6–8
  Irish immigrants to US 4–5
  midget 51
  parades advertising 9
  satire of immigrant groups 53–4
  three-part show 6–7
  in variety houses 30–1, 37, 39
  Westen, H. 79–80
  women performers 6, 30
Mirror 20
M'Liss 36–7
Morris, Lloyd 12
Morse, Salmi: *The Passion* 36
Morton, Charles 131
Motton (performer) 131
Mount, Captain 24
Mount Morris Theatre 36–7
movies 7, 109, 120
Muhman, Harry *14*
music, sheet *44–5*
music halls
  British xiii, xvi, 3, *4*, 4–5, 9, 74; masters of ceremonies 4, 47
  concert saloons known as xi–xii, 3
musical entertainments 18–19, 50–1, 58, 78
  plays 5, 12, 72
  see also orchestras; pianos; songs
"My Son Charlie" (song) 59
Myers, Andrew 54
Myer's Concert Hall 55

Nadel, Stanley 101
navy 91, 102, 104, 108
Neilsen, Alan 22
New Metropolitan Theatre *38*
New Oriental 63, 66, 88, 93
New York Herald 15, 19–20, 37, 42, 62, 120
New Yorker Staats Zeitung 34
Newport, The 28, 51, 52, 127, 128, 130, 131
Niblo's Garden 20
Nieblo's Saloon 101
night clubs 5, 90
nomenclature of concert saloons xi–xii, 3
Novelty Concert Hall 11, 42, 65, 83, 93
number of concert saloons 11
Nym Crinkle 12

Occidental 43, 66, 67, 81
O'Conner; Richard 89

Odell, G. C. D. xx, 15, 19–20, 84
O'Donnell, A. 81
O'Donnell's (Gramercy Hall) 49, 53, 55–6, 71, 81
O'Halloran (performer) 131
Oka-ta-Walla (Indian performer) 16
"Old Arm-Chair, The" (song) 78
Old House at Home 54, 69, 127, 128, 129, 130, 131
olio 6
Olympia, San Francisco 119–20
O'Neill, James 51, 131
opera
    comic 7, 36
    for German audiences 50, 104
opera houses, flat floor 74, 117
Opera Saloon 74, 88, 89, 93–4
orchestras 50, 73, 103
    in dance houses 109, *112*, 113, 116
orchestrion 70, 102, 103
order, keeping of 92, 111, 116
Oriental 20, 23–4, 43, 85, 88, 94
Our Bachelors (comedy) 36
owners and managers 2, 81–2, 104

pageant, *Under the Yoke, Or Bond and Free!* 33
parades 9
Paresis Hall 79
Paris, France 3
Passion, The, banning of 36
Pastor, Tony 8, 40, 47
patrons 82–3, 90–4
performers *see* acts
Phelps 50, 52, 127, 128, 129
Philadelphia, PA 3, 28
phrenologists 74
pianos 42–3, 46, 50, 73, 88
"pick ups" 113, 116
picnic groves 9
pictures in saloons 67–8, 90, 102
"Pitcher of Beer, The" (song) 31
plays, short *see* sketches
pleasure gardens xvi, 5, 7, 8–9
Podhammer (journalist) 62, 65, 78, 80
police 19–20, 23–4, 105, 108
Police Gazette 24, 105, 107, 111, *112*, 113, 116
political satire 56
Post, New York 3–4, 11
post-Civil War period xi–xii, 2, 25, 27–40
poster, stock *71*, 72
Powers, Francis J.: "The First Born" 56
Powers, Madelon xx, 79
premise of sketch 56, 57
premises *see* spaces and equipment
Prescott Hall 85

Presto Hall 68
private rooms or boxes 1, 31, 64, 65, 66–7, 74
prize fights 69, *112*, 113
professional performers 49–50, 77–8, 117, 130–1
programs 58, 64, 120
Prospect Concert Garden 73
prostitutes and prostitution xvii, 9
    accommodation for 1, 74, 75
    concert saloons assumed to offer xi, 1–2, 12, 83–4, 90, 117
    dance houses and 104, 105, 106, 108–9
    employees of concert saloons 26, 41, 59, 90, 105, 117
    entertainments help promote 41, 59
    homosexual 81
    public condemnation xi, 12
    published guides to 84
    theatre managers' attempt to shed connection 91
    waiter girls and 1–2, 83–4, 90, 117
protection money 61
Punch and Judy shows 54, 74, 111, 113
puppet shows 35, 54, 74, 111, 113

Queen, Frank xiv

race *see* ethnic groups
raids, police 23–4, 108
railroads and circus 8
rehearsal 57
Reilly, John F. 120
religion 109, 111
rental halls 29, 33–4
Resorte Musicale 128, 129, 131
Reveille 65–6, 81, 85–6, 87, 92
Rice, T. D. 6
rides, amusement 9
Rivers, Frank 28
Roach, Johnny 62, 131
Robins (senator) 18
rooms, private 1, 66–7, 83
Rosa, Mlle (tight-rope walker) 48
Rose (comic singer) 53, 131
roulette tables 109
"rowdy clubs" 108
Ruppert's 32, 127, 129
Russell, Frank 131
Russell, H. 88

sailors 91, 102, 104, 108
Saint Nicholas Casino 42–3, 85
saloons
    ordinary working men's xiv, 90
    Western 109, 120

Sammy's Bowery Follies 122
San Francisco 36, 119–20
sandwich boards 62
Sans Souci 127, 128, 129
satire 7, 53–4, 55–7
scatological material xvii, 17
Schwab, William 27, 69–70
seats, audience 65
Sells Brothers 8
sets, stage 72
sexuality
    dance houses and 96, 113, 116
    see also prostitutes
"shades, the" 3
Shafer's Eureka 67, 74, 89
shooting galleries 74, 89, 102, 106
shows see acts
sideboards 68
signs, advertising 63–4, 107
Simpson, E. A. 66, 92
Simpson, Matthew 11
sing songs 19, 42–3
singing saloons, British xvi
Sixth Avenue 1, 15
sketches 16, 33, 39, 55–7, 111
"Skids [the Skidmore Guards] Are Out
    Today, The" (song) 50, 128
Slout, William xiv, xix, 3, 20
slump 16–17
Smith family of musicians 46–7, 73
Smith, Leo 131
Smith, Walter 42, 88
Snyder, Robb xix
Society for the Prevention of Juvenile
    Delinquents (SPJD) xiv, xv–xvi, xviii,
    21–4
    and bills: (1839) 22; (Concert, 1862) 22–3;
        (1872) xv, 23, 24, 25–6, 28–40, 48, 60,
        109, 124–6; (amendments of 1875 and
        1876) 32
    challenges from concert saloons to 47–50
    demise 30, 120
    fines paid to 22–3, 28
    and German beer gardens xv, 29, 31–2
    and "legitimate" theatres 29, 35–7
    performers mentioned by 57–60, 78, 130–1
    songs named in reports 127–9
    and variety theatres xv, 29, 37–9
    and young patrons 93
soldiers 12, 17, 18, 27, 40, 91–2, 104
Solomons, Mose 47
"Song and Supper" rooms, British 4
"Song of a Swiper" 41, 47
songs 50, 88–9, 92, 127–9
    sing songs 19, 42–3

sources xiv–xvi
    see also Clipper; Mc Cabe, James Jr; Society
        for the Prevention of Juvenile
        Delinquents
spaces and equipment 30, 61–76
    theatre-like and converted theatres 46, 65
    see also balconies; boxes; costumes; dance
        floors; shooting galleries; stages; and
        under beer gardens, German; dance
        houses
Speyers and Bernheimer's Lager Beer 68
Spirit of the Times 18, 28
SPJD see Society for the Prevention of Juvenile
    Delinquents
sponsored entertainment 9, 33
"Stage Struck" (sketch) 55
stages 1, 69–72, 71, 75–6
    in dance houses 110, 112, 113
    in German beer gardens 98, 101
    in West 117, 120
"Stand By Your Friend" (song) 58
Stanton, Kate 82
Star and Garter 55, 63, 127, 128, 129, 130, 131
Steinway Hall 33, 34
stereoscopes 75
stereotyping 57
stump speeches 6
Stuyvesant, Peter 97
Sukee (performer) 131
Sultan Divan 31
summer gardens 75, 99
Sunday opening 62, 89, 99, 101
"Sunshine After Rain" (song) 88
sweat boxes 109

"Take This Letter to My Mother" (song) 44,
    129
Tambo (minstrel role) 6, 30
tavern shows, British 4
taxi-dancing 104
temperance movement 12
Tenderloin area 15
Tennyson (blackface minstrel) 52, 131
Theatre Comique 55
theatres
    alcohol availability 20–1, 35
    bad reputations 20, 78, 91
    of Bowery 36
    and Concert Bill 91
    converted 73, 107
    rooftop gardens 75, 104
    satirization in concert saloons 56
    small 29, 40, 65
    SPJD investigations 29, 35–7
    see also variety theatres

Theatres Registry Act, British (1843) 4
"theme" establishments 63, 88
"There's a Letter in the Candle" (song) 59
Third Avenue Theatre 36
Times, New York 17–18, 20, 23–4, 79, 96, 99, 101
Tivoli (gambling game) 99
Toby Show 72
Tombstone, Arizona: The Bird Cage 119, *121*
transparencies, advertising 25, 62–3
transvestite as waiter girl 79
Trent, Harrison xiv
Tyrolian Halle 34

"Uncle Josh" 131
Uncle Tom's Cabin shows 79
Under the Yoke, Or Bond and Free!
    (pageant) 33

Valentine's Manual 5
Van Every, Edward 107
Vandermere, Harry 131
Variety magazine 1400
variety theatre xi, 37, *38*, 39
    acts 37, *38*, 39
    and burlesque 37
    in Civil War slump 16–17
    concert saloon acts with origins in 49, 60
    concert saloons with premises similar to 65
    confusion of concert saloons with xiii, xiv, 9
    minstrels in 7, 39
    SPJD's investigations xv, 29, 37–9
    and vaudeville 37
vaudeville 7, 37, 40
    cs as precursor xi, xiii, 5, 9
Victoria, Mlle 131
"Violet from My Mother's Grave, A" (song)
    31, 129
Virginia Minstrels, The 6
Volksgarten 99, 101

waiter girls xvii, 1, 9, 83–90
    and alcohol sales 86
    allegations of immorality xi, 1–2, 20, 83–4,
        90, 117
    book depicting faces of 19, 84
    Concert Bill and 42, 77
    costumes 87–8
    end of fashion for xix, 2, 23, 26, 29, 31, 40,
        41, 57, 83
    male transvestite 79
    pay 85–6

performances by 43, 88–9, 92
poem on 77
poster showing *71, 72*
and prostitution 1–2, 83–4, 90, 117
rules for 86
in West 117, 118
waiters, male 80–1, 120
Wallace, Mike xix
Wallack's theatre 20, 35, 78
Walters, Charles 59
Warren, John 86–7
Washington, DC 77, 117
Washington, George 101–2, 103
Water Street, dance hall in 108–9
Waters, Charles 131
Weaver, Dan 59, 131
West
    concert saloons xi, 74, 109, 117–20;
        motion-picture stereotype 109, 120
    flat floor opera houses 117
Westen, Horace 58, 62, 79–80, 131
What Is It, Ballard's 42, 61, 63, 75, 90, 92
Wheeler, Professor (phrenologist) 74
White, Charlie 47
White Fawn, The (musical play) 5
Wilkes' *Spirit of the Times* 18, 28
Williams, Pete 108
Williamsburg, Brooklyn 97
Wilton's Music Hall, London *4*
Windsor Gardens 52–3
Winter Garden 20, 110, 127, 130, 131
winter gardens 99
women
    black, in dance houses 108
    and immorality 2, 12, 17–18, 20
    owners of establishments 82, 104
    patrons 28, 82, 83
    performers xvii, 1, 51, 78, 82, 103, 118–19;
        ballet girls 20, 85; minstrels 6, 30; waiter
        girls as 43, 88–9, 92
    satirization of 57
    see also prostitutes; waiter girls
Worrell Sisters 39
wrestling matches 54

Yiddish entertainments 101, 104
Yorkville, Manhattan 97, 99
young people 92–3, 101

Zeke (freak) 63
Zellers, Parker xix–xx, 28